# AA Explore

# THE HEART OF ENGLAND

*How Hill, a haven for wildlife in the heart of The Broads*

AA Publishing

Text and illustrations taken from the series *Explore Britain's...*, first published by the Automobile Association and the Daily Telegraph in 1993 and 1995:

*Explore Britain's Castles* by Elizabeth Cruwys and Beau Riffenburg
*Explore Britain's Coastline* by Richard Cavendish
*Explore Britain's Country* Gardens by Michael Wright
*Explore Britain's Historic Houses* by Penny Hicks
*Explore Britain's National Parks* by Roland Smith
*Explore Britain's Steam Railways* by Anthony Lambert
*Explore Britain's Villages* by Susan Gordon

Published by AA Publishing, a trading name of Automobile Association Developments Limited, whose registered office is Norfolk House, Priestley Road, Basingstoke, Hampshire RG24 9NY. Registered Number 1878835.

© The Automobile Association 1996

Maps © Advanced Illustration, Congleton 1996

A catalogue record for this book is available from the British Library.

ISBN 0 7495 1302 0

Colour origination by L.C. Repro & Sons Ltd, Aldermaston, England
Printed and bound in Italy by Tipolitografia G. Canale & C.S.p.A. – Turin

The contents of this book are believed correct at the time of printing. Nevertheless, the Publishers cannot accept responsibility for errors or omissions, or for changes in details given.

Acknowledgements

AA PHOTO LIBRARY B/Cover: a, c S. & O. Mathews, b, e M. Birkitt, d C. Mellor, f W. Voysey; 1 A. Souter; 3 M. Birkitt; 7 L. Whitwam; 9 C. Mellor; 10/11, 11, 12, 13 A. Tryner; 14 M. Adleman; 15 V. Greaves; 16/17 F. Stephenson; 18 V. Greaves; 19 R. Newton; 20, 21, 22, 23a, b C. Mellor; 24 F. Stephenson; 25 R. Newton; 26/7 A. Tryner; 28, 29 M. Birkitt; 30, 30/1 P. Baker; 32 A. Tryner; 33 P. Baker; 34 A. Tryner; 35, 36 P. Baker; 37 A. Tryner; 38 T. Woodcock, 39 R. Surman; 40/1 P. Baker, 42 V. Greaves, 43 A. Tryner, 44 R. Newton; 45; 46; 47; 48; 49 A. Tryner, 50 P. Baker, 52 T. Woodcock, 53 A. Tryner, 54 R. Newton, 54/5; 56 A. Tryner, 57 R. Newton, 58; 59 M. Birkitt; 60 V. Greaves; 61 A. Lawson; 62/3, 63, 64 M. Birkitt; 65 A. Tryner; 66, 67, 68/9a, 68/9b M. Birkitt; 71 P. Baker; 72 M. Birkitt; 73 R. Surman; 74 D. Forss; 75 H. Williams; 76 P. Baker; 77 A. Souter; 78, 79, 80/1, 81, 82 M. Birkitt; 83 R. J. Edwards; 84, 85 A. Souter; 86/7, 87 M. Birkitt; 90 A. Souter; 91a S. & O. Mathews; 91b A. Souter; 92 A. J. Hopkins; 94/5, 95 R. J. Edwards; 96/7 A. Perkins; 98/9 A. Souter; 99, 100 A. Perkins; 100/1 S. & O. Mathews; 102, 102/3, 104/5 A. Perkins; 105, 106, 107, 108 S. & O. Mathews; 109 R. Surman; 110, 111 A. Perkins; 112/3, 114 S. & O. Mathews; 115 M. Trelawny; 116, 117a, b M. Birkitt; 118 T. Woodcock; 119 S. & O. Mathews; 120 W. Voysey; 121, 122, 123 S. & O. Mathews; 124, 125 M. Birkitt; 126/7, 126, 127 P. Davies
HADDON HALL 51
DAVID LEE/THE NATIONAL TRUST 8
MANNINGTON GARDENS & COUNTRYSIDE 88/9
ANDY WILLIAMS PHOTO LIBRARY F/Cover Welford upon Avon

# CONTENTS

# HEART OF ENGLAND

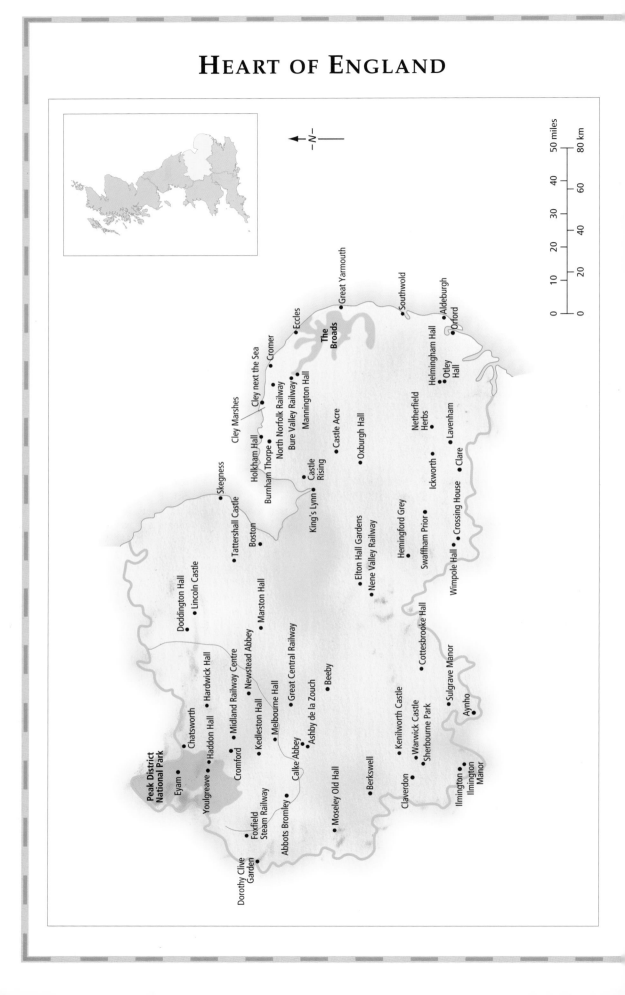

– N –

50 miles
80 km

Great Yarmouth
Southwold
Aldeburgh
Orford
Eccles
Cromer
Helmingham Hall
Otley Hall
Cley next the Sea
The Broads
Cley Marshes
North Norfolk Railway
Bure Valley Railway
Holkham Hall
Mannington Hall
Netherfield Herbs
Burnham Thorpe
Castle Acre
Oxburgh Hall
Lavenham
Skegness
Castle Rising
King's Lynn
Ickworth
Clare
Tattershall Castle
Boston
Elton Hall Gardens
Nene Valley Railway
Hemingford Grey
Swaffham Prior
Crossing House
Wimpole Hall
Doddington Hall
Lincoln Castle
Marston Hall
Cottesbrooke Hall
Hardwick Hall
Midland Railway Centre
Newstead Abbey
Great Central Railway
Beeby
Sulgrave Manor
Chatsworth
Haddon Hall
Kedleston Hall
Melbourne Hall
Ashby de la Zouch
Aynho
Peak District National Park
Eyam
Cromford
Calke Abbey
Kenilworth Castle
Warwick Castle
Sherbourne Park
Youlgreave
Foxfield Steam Railway
Moseley Old Hall
Berkswell
Claverdon
Ilmington
Ilmington Manor
Dorothy Clive Garden
Abbots Bromley

# ꞨNTRODUCTION

*Stands the Church clock at ten to three?*
*And is there honey still for tea?*

Rupert Brooke, 'The Old Vicarage, Grantchester'

Stretching from just beyond the Welsh border counties, right across to East Anglia, the Heart of England is naturally an area of great diversity: serene valleys, elegant stately houses and castles, historic market towns, bustling fishing ports, picture postcard villages and much more.

'The slopes of wold and valley are dotted with copses and noble trees, amongst which lie tiny villages and square-towered churches...Beyond the eastern range of hills lies the marsh, a flat strip of rich pasture land about five to eight miles wide, divided up into fields by broad ditches, which are filled in summer with tall, feathery reeds. Beyond this is the North Sea, peculiar for the long rise and fall of the tide over the flat sandy shore and fringed by a line of high sand dunes...' Charles Tennyson's words may describe the Lincolnshire landscape near Somersby, birthplace of his grandfather, Alfred Lord Tennyson, but how suited they could be for the whole of this area.

Delight in the tranquillity of The Broads, an enchanting, but incredibly, man-made network of mysterious fens and meandering waterways; a haven for birds and other wildlife. Visit proud villages like Eyam, steeped in history, whose villagers so bravely isolated themselves from the outside world to prevent the spread of plague across the country, a sacrifice which cost them dearly: surely showing enough heart for the whole region .

*The stately homes of England,*
*How beautiful they stand!*
*Amidst their tall ancestral trees,*
*O'er all the pleasant land.*

'The Homes of England' by Felicia Dorothea Hemans

(1793–1835)

# MOSELEY OLD HALL
## *Staffordshire*

### 3½ MILES (5.5 KM) NORTH OF WOLVERHAMPTON

*I*n one of the least promising parts of Wolverhampton you suddenly come upon the truly remarkable Moseley Old Hall, set in its equally amazing garden. From the outside, the house belies its age, but as soon as you enter it is clear that this is a timber-framed Tudor manor house – and indeed, it is the building in which the future Charles II took refuge after his defeat at the Battle of Worcester in 1651. When the property was given to the National Trust in 1962 it was in a bad condition, and the 1 acre (0.5ha) garden was virtually non-existent. Within a very short time, however, Graham Stuart Thomas, assisted by Miles Hadfield, had recreated the garden in the mid-17th-century style,

*An excellent view of the formal knot garden, with its trimmed trees and neatly raked gravel*

which, now fully matured, forms the wonderful layout we see today.

The main feature of the garden is the knot which lies to the south of the Hall and is best seen from its upper windows. A copy of one designed by the Reverend Walter Stonehouse in 1640, it consists of 11 clipped spheres of box standing on 3ft (1m) stems surrounded by circular gravel beds edged with dwarf box hedges. Along one side of the knot is an arbour now draped with the fragrant *Clematis flammula*, the white-flowering virgin's bower, and *Clematis viticella*, making a contrast with the deep-purple Teinturier grape, while narrow borders are filled with strongly scented lavender.

*In complete contrast, an informal flower border is set against the old wall*

The arbour leads through a hornbeam tunnel to the Nut Alley, lined on each side with different varieties of snowdrops, winter aconites and the Siberian squill flower in early spring. These are succeeded by the stinking hellebores and by snake's head fritillary, followed in autumn by colchicums and pink-flowering cyclamens. At the end of the alley is the gate through which Charles Stuart is supposed to have entered secretly, and in the field beyond is one sweet chestnut, all that remains from the Long Walk. The flagged path leading to the back door is lined with morello cherries, quinces, black mulberries and medlars. At the far end is a small herb garden enclosed by box, with a fragrant mock orange underplanted with Lenten roses.

The front garden, once a paved court, now consists of lawns with spirals and cones of box, and two beds of tutsan edged by *Teucrium chamaedrys*. The mixed borders against the walls are filled with splendid herbs like Solomon's seal, red valerian, the pink and white varieties of *Paeonia officianalis*, and the lovely garden herb soapwort, the soapy sap of which is nowadays used in museums for laundering and revitalising precious fabrics. Moseley Old Hall is an enchanting garden, full of interesting plants that were once grown for medicinal and cleaning purposes and to provide dyes.

Open on selected days from April to October. Tel: 01902 782808.

# FOXFIELD STEAM RAILWAY
## *Staffordshire*

### BLYTHE BRIDGE, 6 MILES (9.5 KM) SOUTH-EAST OF STOKE-ON-TRENT

*Opposite: on the Foxfield line – a surprisingly rural and scenic route for a former colliery railway*

A former colliery railway in the heart of the Staffordshire coalfield might seem to appeal to none but the most avid enthusiast, but don't be put off – the views from these trains are a far cry from bleak post-industrial landscapes. The spoil tips from the colliery are now largely overgrown, and for most of the journey the line passes through woods that threaten to engulf the train, so close do the branches come, or past fields of grazing cows or corn. In the distance the fringes of the Staffordshire moors can be seen, and across the valley is the village after which the line named its northern terminus, Dilhorne. It is denoted by the octagonal spire of All Saints' church.

Until the number of British coal mines was decimated, most collieries were connected to the railway system by sidings or by a branch line. Most of these have been built over or returned to nature, but close to Blythe Bridge station on the Stoke–Derby line is a surviving branch that served a mine in the once prosperous Staffordshire coalfield. Coal was mined at Foxfield in the 17th century, but it was 1893 before a branch was built off the North Staffordshire Railway, known locally as the 'Knotty' after the county emblem it adopted. The mine closed in 1965 but a 2¾-mile (4.5km) section was saved by a group of enthusiasts. The final part to the mine itself did not become part of the Foxfield Light Railway, and this is a great shame because it had the steepest gradient and the mine buildings could have formed an interesting feature.

This loss prompted the group to establish a new station, engine shed and museum at the opposite end of the line close to Blythe Bridge. Visitors usually have a look round the collection of locomotives before taking a ride – all are tank engines and were once employed in industrial use, some of them in the Midland counties. Perhaps most surprising on a former colliery railway is the provision of a bar and observation car, known as

the Bass Belle, which provides welcome refreshment and helps the railway's coffers.

The small size of most of the Foxfield's locomotives means that they have to work hard pulling the former British Railways carriages, but try to visit on one of the special days, when there is a demonstration of coal wagons being worked up the 1 in 25 gradient from the colliery. These demonstrations provide a spectacle and sound that are unforgettable.

Train service: from Easter to September, Sundays and Bank Holiday weekends. Santa specials. Tel: 01782 396210.

# THE DOROTHY CLIVE GARDEN

*Staffordshire*

WILLOUGHBRIDGE, 9 MILES (14.5 KM) NORTH-EAST OF MARKET DRAYTON

*The cascading waterfall is a distinctive feature of this famous garden*

Situated in the splendid rolling countryside on the border between Staffordshire and Shropshire, the Dorothy Clive Gardens were designed and laid out by Colonel Harry Clive as a memorial to his wife. The gardens now cover 7 acres (3ha), but the garden built by the Clives in the 1930s was much smaller. It was when his wife became too infirm to do more than make a circuit of the lawns that Colonel Clive conceived the idea of creating a woodland garden from a $1^1/_2$ acre (0.5ha) gravel pit, which had been left undisturbed for more than 20 years and consequently was a dense mass of pines, small oaks, silver birches, brambles and holly. Paths were cut through the undergrowth and rhododendrons

planted, and today this magical, enclosed area is a riot of spring colour. Every shade of red, pink, purple, mauve and yellow can be seen, and among the more interesting plants are the blood-red *Rhododendron thompsonii*, rose-pink *R. orbiculare* with its heart-shaped leaves, and the hybrids *R.* 'Sappho' and *R.* 'Goldsworth Yellow'. As the rhododendrons begin to fade, hybrid azaleas, including 'Exbury' and 'Ghent', blossom and fill the air with their heady scent.

After Dorothy Clive's death in 1942, Colonel Clive sold their house, Elds Gorse, and set up a garden trust based at a new bungalow constructed at the entrance to the quarry. He then began to develop the land that sloped down

to the road. A collection of Exbury azaleas were planted, and to celebrate his 80th birthday, his grandchildren planted two blue cedars, *Cedrus atlantica glauca*. Since Colonel Clive's death in 1963 the gardens have been extended, and a rock and scree garden has been a recent addition. Here dwarf tulips and a great many spring bulbs can be seen, while, around the pool, irises and candelabra primulas flourish. In summer, angel's fishing rods show their purplish-red flowers, and ligularias their yellow and orange flowers against green and purple foliage.

Island beds in the lawn contain a wonderful selection of herbaceous plants, shrubs and roses. Along the western edge of the garden is a collection of more than 80 camellias, while heather captures the eye below the striking bark of silver birches.

This garden shows colour at all times of the year. Winter aconites are among the first to appear, followed by crocuses, including *Crocus tommasinianus* with its lavender-coloured flowers. After the rhododendrons are over, the shrub roses provide eye-catching colour, to be followed by gazanias, osteospermums and crocosmias. Dahlias and chrysanthemums begin the autumn season, and, with the elegant pink flowers of the late-flowering *Nerine bowdenii*, the year at Dorothy Clive comes to an end.

Open from April to October, daily. Tel: 01630 647237.

*The lower section of the garden, including the lily pond, was designed by John Codrington*

**Ancient Rites**

The antlers used for the Horn Dance have been carbon dated to Norman times but, although the dance seems to have been connected with the church since medieval days, there are elements that suggest much earlier, pre-Christian rituals. Maid Marian, a man dressed as a woman, for example, hints at ancient fertility rites, while the bowman stalking the deer men is reminiscent of a Stone Age painting in the Lascaux Caves depicting bowmen in pursuit of men wearing antlers on their heads.

*The butter cross and the Goat's Head Inn*

# ABBOTS BROMLEY
## *Staffordshire*

### 5 MILES (8 KM) NORTH-EAST OF RUGELEY

*I*t is for its ancient Horn Dance, performed early in September, that the name of Abbots Bromley is familiar to many. But the village has plenty to beguile the visitor in other months too, particularly enthusiasts of timber-framing. At the centre of this one-time market town the hexagonal butter cross building marks where local farmers used to trade their produce. Close by is the black and white panelled Goat's Head Inn and the brick-built Bagot Almshouses, endowed in 1705 by the local family who have lived for 500 years in nearby Blithfield Hall. The public school, St Mary and St Anne's, is housed in a clump of buildings behind the lofty 1881 chapel on the high street, while the village school house of 1606 is another half-timbered building, behind a Victorian successor in Schoolhouse Lane. In a number of houses timber-framing is concealed behind brick, but there is nothing to hide the glory of Church House, whose particularly fanciful timberwork is typical of the West Midlands. The church is restored medieval, and it is here that the reindeer horns used for the Horn Dance are kept. Six deer men carry the horns and perform this ancient ritual, of uncertain origin, in and around the village, accompanied by a fool, a hobby horse, a bowman and the man-woman, Maid Marian.

# BERKSWELL
## *West Midlands*

### 6 MILES (9.5 KM) WEST OF COVENTRY

**B**erk, or as he was known to the Anglo Saxons Bercol, owned a well here in the Forest of Arden, in which the King of the Mercians was baptised by the monks of Lichfield. This large square stone well is behind the brick, Victorian almshouses that face the green. The king went on to build a small church here, providing it with a large crypt. When the Normans rebuilt the church in the 12th century, they reconstructed this crypt and built another one alongside. They are exceptional. There is a very good Norman chancel, a monument by Westmacott decorated with roses and voluptuous angels, and several woodcarver-Thompson mouse trademarks. Outside, the south doorway is sheltered by a half-timbered porch with a room over, its grey timbers set off by the pinkish sandstone walls of this lovely church. The adjoining 17th-century old rectory is stone-faced and has prettily shaped gables. There is some thatch and some timber-framing in the village, including the 400-year-old Bear Inn outside which stands a cannon from the Crimean War. On the green itself are the old stocks. Why do they have five holes, is the puzzle. Was it to accommodate a particular one-legged reprobate alongside his two mates? Or, perhaps, has a sixth hole rotted away?

A hobby horse is, unexpectedly, housed in the church porch. It is said to have been used by an 18th-century huntsman parson who felt able to preach only when on horseback.

*In a village that once supported a brick-making industry, mellow brick walls are a foil to a pretty cottage garden*

Sir Walter Scott's novel *Kenilworth* was published in 1821. It tells of events that were supposed to have occurred during the visit of Elizabeth I to the castle in 1575.

# KENILWORTH CASTLE
## *Warwickshire*

### KENILWORTH, 5 MILES (8 KM) SOUTH-WEST OF COVENTRY

The deep red stones of one of Britain's mightiest keeps was the scene of one of the most important sieges in English history. In 1238 a young French noble, who had claimed a tenuous hold on the earldom of Leicester, secretly married King Henry III's recently widowed sister. The young noble was Simon de Montfort, and during the next 27 years he would become one of Henry's greatest friends and most bitter enemies. Henry gave Kenilworth to his brother-in-law in 1244, but later de Montfort voiced his opposition to the absolute power of the monarchy and openly declared war on the king, making Kenilworth his rebel headquarters. At first, many nobles were struck by the sense of de Montfort's proposals, and they flocked to his cause. Even Henry's son Edward, heir to the throne of England, took de Montfort's side against his father at first. When he eventually changed sides, de Montfort imprisoned him at Kenilworth Castle. Edward escaped and played a vital

role in the defeat and death of de Montfort at the Battle of Lewes in 1265.

De Montfort's supporters fled to Kenilworth, where the rebellion continued under his son. The siege that was to follow lasted six months, and was perhaps one of the most violent ever to take place on English soil. Because the castle was protected on three sides by water, the attackers could not undermine the walls and had to concentrate instead on trying to breach the great defences of the gatehouse and walls. Contemporary accounts tell how besiegers and besieged hurled missiles at each other from great war machines. So intense was this fire, that the stones exploded as they crashed into each other in mid-air. The castle was finally overcome by starvation, not because the castle could no longer be defended.

The first castle at Kenilworth was a simple mound with wooden buildings, and the magnificent keep was not raised until the 12th century. It was a massive building, with an entrance on the first floor that was protected by a substantial forebuilding. Robert Dudley, Earl of Leicester, was responsible for changing the narrow windows into large ones that would flood the upper chambers with light. Dudley was the favourite of Elizabeth I, and he lived in constant expectation of a visit from her. He built a fine gatehouse and a graceful residential suite, intended specifically for the Queen.

Much has survived of this important castle. The great red keep looms powerfully over the elegant 16th-century residences, all still protected by strong walls, earthworks and the great mere.

Open all year daily, except Christmas and New Year. Tel: 01926 52078.

*Below, although Cromwell ordered Kenilworth to be demolished, enough remains today to show what a magnificent fortress it must have been*

# ILMINGTON
*Warwickshire*

### 4 MILES (6.5 KM) NORTH-WEST OF SHIPSTON ON STOUR

A tangle of lanes and alleyways, golden houses with mullioned windows and stone roofs, old cottage gardens, far-reaching views – even Morris dancing. Ilmington has everything needed to make it one of the county's show pieces; it is in that part of Warwickshire that seems to jab cheekily into Gloucestershire and Oxfordshire and shares all the Cotswold hallmarks. There is a chalybeate spring, which in the late 19th century turned the place into something of a spa for a while. A large pool at the northern end of the village is the site of fish ponds which belonged to the manor opposite. The manor was built in the 16th century with fine gables and mullioned windows looking on to its lovely garden. Footpaths lead to the church below the upper green. It has a chunky Norman tower and zig-zagged doorway. Inside, it feels wide, with hefty arches to the tower and chancel. The Victorian old school building, with bell-cote, is now a Roman Catholic church, while at the western end of the upper green is stone-built Crab Mill, dated to 1711. Facing on to the lower of the two greens is the shop and The Howard Inn, named after one of the leading families of the area who lived in Foxcote House, an early Georgian mansion a little out of the village.

*Summer sunshine brings out the warmth of the Cotswold stone*

**Great Gardens**

Just 2 or 3 miles away, over the border with Gloucestershire, are two glorious Cotswold gardens, Hidcote Manor Garden (National Trust), a series of small gardens created by the great horticulturist Lawrence Johnston, and Kiftsgate Court Garden, noted for its collection of old-fashioned roses. Both are open to the public from spring to autumn.

*The old forge*

# CLAVERDON
## *Warwickshire*

### 6 MILES (9.5 KM) WEST OF WARWICK

Claverdon, or Clover Down, is an ancient village set on a hill overlooking the Warwickshire countryside. With its ready access to the M40 and a reprieved railway station, its attractions are not lost to property developers and recent years have brought considerable growth, but at its centre there are some fine old buildings. The church, of greyish stone, was built in the 15th century but partly reconstructed during the 19th century. Here is the tomb of Sir Thomas Spencer (*d.*1630), lord of the manor. His house was demolished some 30 years after his death, though the stone tower-house of the Hall is said to have been part of it. Also in the church is a tablet commemorating Francis Galton, FRS (1822–1911), grandson of Erasmus Darwin and cousin of Charles. He studied heredity and it was he who established that fingerprints are permanent and unique. He was also the first to construct serious weather charts. The most unusual building in the village has to be the old forge, a half-timbered building with an entirely appropriate doorway. Park Farm and its cottages are also timber-framed. The mid-19th century school buildings, in contrast, have an Italianate air.

# ILMINGTON MANOR
## *Warwickshire*

ILMINGTON, 4 MILES (6.5 KM) NORTH-WEST OF SHIPSTON-ON-STOUR

*The sundial, adrift in a sea of gentle grey foliage and soft pink roses*

Few who visit the lovely gardens of Ilmington Manor today would guess that they are only 70 years old. When the late Mr Spenser Flower came to this magical village in 1919, the honey-coloured stone manor house dating from 1600 had become a place for squatters, and an orchard occupied the position of the present garden. With a flair for design and with a clear idea of what he wanted, Mr Flower restored and enlarged his new home, and then, with the help of his wife, who was a keen plantswoman, set about creating the interesting and beautiful garden that we see today.

To the right of the drive, which is lined with hornbeams, is a little Pond Garden. The edges of the tank itself were decorated with carved stone panels that Mr Flower had found and considered to be Jacobean, and the surrounding paving is overgrown with many different varieties of scented thyme. The beds are filled with pink diascea, dianthus and other sun-lovers, while trailing sedums continue the patterns on the walls of the pool. This attractive area is bounded to the north and east by walls draped with clematis, a fine banksia rose and other aromatic climbers, but it is a surprise to find *Buddleia crispa*, as this has a reputation for tenderness.

The Pillar Borders are separated by a grass walk and present a most unusual combination of shrubs and herbaceous plants carefully arranged in colour groups.

Steps lead into the formal Rose Garden, among two long borders planted with old and modern shrub roses. 'Madame Hardy' and 'Scarlet Fire' can be seen, as can 'Louise Odier', 'Cerise Bouquet' and 'Charles de Mills', while there are modern long-flowering specimens such as 'Arthur Bell' and 'Scented Air'. Beyond three large walnut trees and a dovecote perched high above a neatly clipped hedge are drifts of naturalised daffodils and brightly coloured crocuses in spring. A low, circular rock garden built of local limestone partly encloses the orchard, and the other side is flanked by imposing shrubs and beautiful herbaceous plants.

The so-called Dutch Garden is in one of the most colourful parts of

Ilmington Manor – although this is really more of an informal cottage garden. Designed by the present owner, Mr D Flower's cousin, Lady Flower, it features the most enchanting mixture of roses, lavender and scented mock oranges, and peonies and hardy geraniums stand alongside clematis-

clad walls. Large varieties of lily such as *Lilium regale* and *L. speciosum rubrum* make a dramatic appearance, while hemerocallis and agapanthus grow together. In Lady Flower's White Border artemisias and senecios compete with white penstemons and variegated laurustinus. Although the design of this garden must have been influenced by Lawrence Johnston's Hidcote (see page 38), which is only a few miles away, it is very individual, and will give constant pleasure and delight however often it is visited.

Open on selected days from May to July, and by appointment. Tel: 01608 682230.

*A corner of the colourful Dutch Garden*

---

# SHERBOURNE PARK
## *Warwickshire*

### SHERBOURNE, 3 MILES (5 KM) SOUTH OF WARWICK

---

*Above, a section of the parterre*

*Right above, the church is drawn into the garden, domminating the view*

*Right below, the charming red-brick house, which pre-dates the garden by nearly 100 years*

I has long been a tradition of English garden-making that the layout should respond to, and draw its inspiration from, its countryside setting. Nowhere is this consistency more apparent than in the lovely gardens of Sherbourne Park. Set deep in lush countryside with fine views over farmland to the River Avon, and adjacent to Sherbourne Church – built in 1863 by Sir George Gilbert Scott – the red-brick house was built in early Georgian times by Smith of Warwick.

When the Smith-Rylands came to live at Sherbourne Park in 1953 there was little in the way of a garden, and one of the first steps was to create a ha-ha to protect the garden from straying cattle while preserving the views, not least the one of the new avenue of poplars, centred on the house but planted outside the ditch. The tall tower of the church has almost been incorporated into the garden too, as it dominates the views over the L-shaped lake from the main terrace and from the Bottom Garden. The construction of a swimming pool on the south side of the house in 1960 prompted the creation of a series of beautiful 'garden rooms' by the designer of the layout, Lady Smith-Ryland.

Immediately outside the house a paved terrace is now covered by clematis, wisteria and a *Magnolia grandiflora*, with fuchsias growing in terracotta pots. The pool pavilion gives shelter to a border which boasts

*Mahonia x media* 'Charity', and, inside the enclosure itself, beds contain honeysuckle, agapanthus, nerines and an old rose, 'Bennett's Seedling', trained on the wall. Down a flight of steps is the Bottom Garden, planted like an orchard except that the trees are sorbus. The far end of this area is screened by golden and green yews into which *Rosa longicuspis* and 'Paul's Himalayan Musk' have been allowed to climb. A simple parterre has been created close to the churchyard wall, the beds edged with box and filled with roses, grey-leaved herbs and perennials, with honeysuckle in the corners.

The White Garden is surrounded by yew hedges with four *Juniperus virginiana* 'Skyrocket' dominating the central bed, while other borders contain philadelphus, rock roses, lychnis, delphiniums, geraniums and anthemis. Beyond, there is a way through a garden with a group of weeping pears to an arboretum with ailanthus, beeches, whitebeam, *Salix matsudana* and *Cedrus deodara*. There is yet another garden to the east of the house and that too reinforces the link, so apparent at Sherbourne Park, between the garden and the surrounding countryside.

Open on selected afternoons and by appointment. Tel: 01926 624255.

*The view of Warwick Castle across the willow fringed River Avon was said by Sir Walter Scott to be unsurpassed in England*

## ❊
# WARWICK CASTLE
## *Warwickshire*

### WARWICK, 3 MILES (5 KM) FROM LEAMINGTON SPA
❊

One of the most unpopular figures in 14th-century England was the grasping Piers Gaveston. Gaveston was the son of a Gascon knight, and attracted the attentions of Edward II long before he became king. Edward lavished titles and riches on his favourite, thereby antagonising his barons into open hostility, both against Gaveston and the King himself. Several attempts were made to banish Gaveston, but none had any lasting success. Then, in 1312, desperate measures were taken when Guy, the Earl of Warwick, and other barons seized Gaveston and took him to Warwick Castle. There, perhaps in the Great Hall, Gaveston was given a perfunctory trial and sentenced to death. He was executed on Blacklow Hill, just outside Warwick.

The powerful walls of Warwick Castle tower over the River Avon and the surrounding countryside. Because the castle has been constantly occupied since the Normans first erected a mound here, many fine buildings have been added over the centuries. Among the most magnificent are the imposing Jacobean wing and the 14th-century Guy's Tower. Inside the castle are many splendid rooms, including the State Rooms with their lavish furnishings, as well as a tasteful tableau of wax figures to recreate an actual late 19th century house party. There is an outstanding collection of arms and armour, as well as a new 'sights and sounds' exhibition, 'Warwick the Kingmaker'.

Open all year, daily except Christmas. Tel: 01926 408000.

# MELBOURNE HALL
## *Derbyshire*

### MELBOURNE, 9 MILES (14.5 KM) SOUTH OF DERBY

*A* fine, elegant mansion standing in celebrated grounds and gardens, Melbourne Hall has had a chequered history which goes back to the 12th century. Originally the residence of the Bishops of Carlisle, it was later committed to the hands of a succession of lessees who sadly neglected the building. By the time Sir Francis Needham purchased the lease he found it necessary to demolish and rebuild a large part of the Hall, thus creating the grand house which exists today.

Sir John Coke was the next owner and his descendant, Lord Ralph Kerr, and his family are still at Melbourne, providing the warm and comfortable lived-in atmosphere which so delights visitors. The house is beautifully furnished and contains many fine works of art.

There are some notable characters associated with the history of Melbourne – mostly from the Lamb family, who became Lords Melbourne – with stories of doubtful parentage and moral lassitude. Lady Caroline Lamb, wife of the 2nd Viscount Melbourne, had a famous affair with Lord Byron which led to formal separation from her husband in 1825. The 2nd Viscount was to become Queen Victoria's first Prime Minister; he also gave his name to the Australian city. Another Victorian Prime Minister later owned Melbourne – Lord Palmerston, who was married to Emily Lamb.

Open daily during August. Tel: 01332 862502.

*The gardens of Melbourne Hall were laid out in the 18th century in the style of Le Nôtre*

# PEAK DISTRICT

The Peak District, sandwiched between the great industrial cities of northern England, was the first British National Park to be designated in 1951. It was an area where a National Park was most needed, subjected, as it still is, to incredible pressures from mineral extraction, development and public access. The Peak, standing at the foot of the Pennines, is at the crossroads of Britain on the transition zone between the highlands and the lowlands. Because of this it is a paradise for the naturalist, with wildlife from widely differing habitats coexisting side by side in a precious but pressurised island of sharply contrasting landscapes.

*Above, looking east down the valley of Edale from Rushup Edge, with Kinder Scout on the left*

*Right, A dry day at Kinder Downfall, the great waterfall on the western edge of Kinder Scout*

*Previous pages, Shutlingsloe, one of the few real peaks in the Peak District, from Shining Tor*

*I*'ll never forget my first visit to Kinder Scout, at 2,088ft (636m) the highest point of the 555 square mile (1,438 sq km) Peak National Park. The day wasn't promising. A thick grey blanket of cloud (known as 'clag' in these parts) lay heavily over the tops as we drove into the green valley of Edale to the start of the walk. However, as we had come a long way and were well equipped with map and compass we thought we'd give it a go.

The climb up from the typical little Pennine hamlet of Upper Booth, originally a Tudor cattle herdsman's shelter or vaccary, was pleasant enough and the weather even started to brighten – as it often can in these hills. There were occasional brief showers as we climbed steeply, accompanied by the constantly chattering Crowden Brook. Above us to the left, frowning down on the valley like the bastion of some medieval castle, stood Crowden Tower, one of Kinder's famous gritstone tors. The path disappeared in a jumble of rocks at the head of the clough as we struggled upwards, scrambling over enormous gritstone blocks and terraces to eventually emerge, sweating but triumphant, at the top. The scene which greeted our unbelieving eyes was staggering, and

it took what little of our breath was left clean away.

Before us as far as the eye could see stretched the most amazingly wild moonscape that either of us had ever seen. Wave after wave of banks of chocolate-brown peat, gently steaming in the now-strong sunlight, rolled away to the distant horizon, looking for all the world like a petrified ocean of manure.

John Hillaby, doyen of walking writers, described it perfectly in his *Journey Through Britain*. In a chapter entitled 'The Kinder Caper', he wrote: 'The top of Kinder Scout looks as if it's entirely covered in the droppings of dinosaurs'. The analogy, as far as we could see, was perfect.

When we'd got our breath back we walked west through the jumble of huge boulders behind Crowden Tower into another of Kinder's many surprises, known on the map as The Woolpacks. This amazing collection of weirdly shaped gritstone tors – some surrounded by a moat, others resembling anvils, chairs, toadstools, and even recumbent animals – is also known as Whipsnade and the Mushroom Garden, and it was easy to see why. In mist, these smooth, natural sculptures can take on a brooding, primeval quality which gives them a life of their own.

appropriately known as bogtrotters – a new and entirely unexpected aspect.

There are really two distinct Peak Districts – two areas of equally beautiful but totally different landscapes, each of which has its own avid supporters. Kinder and the northern moors of Bleaklow and Black Hill, whose very names give away their hard, masculine nature, form the biggest block of what is known as the Dark Peak. The Dark Peak spreads around the northern, western and eastern sides of the National Park like an upturned horseshoe, while the softer, more feminine landscape of the White Peak occupies the centre and the south. It is a distinction based on the underlying geology of the area, for the

*Chatsworth House, stately home of the Duke of Devonshire and known as the Palace of the Peak, with the Emperor Fountain*

As we climbed down the ancient packhorse route of Jacob's Ladder, named not after the biblical figure but much more prosaically after Jacob Marshall, a local farmer who first cut the steps into the hillside in the 17th century, we reflected that Kinder was certainly different and unlike anywhere else we'd been in Britain. I have climbed up Kinder's craggy sides many times since then, and every time I see or experience something entirely different. That is the attraction of Kinder Scout and the high northern moors of the Peak District – they always have this magnificent sense of age-old permanence, yet on every visit they show their devotees –

Dark Peak moors, tors and edges (escarpments) are formed by sombre-coloured millstone grit and the White Peak plateau and dales from pearly-white limestone. Both rocks are sedimentary, laid down during the carboniferous period about 350 million years ago when the land we now know as Britain was much closer to the equator.

The limestone is the fossilised remains of countless millions of tiny sea creatures and organisms which were laid down in a shallow, semi-tropical sea. This was later overlaid with mud and grit deposited by a huge prehistoric river, forming the grits, shales and sandstones of the Dark Peak. Countless millions of years

of erosion by wind, water and ice have gradually and remorselessly removed the gritstone cover from the centre and south of the Peak, revealing the dazzling white limestone skeleton beneath. This is all the stuff of textbook geology, making the Peak a popular place for students of that science.

However, you don't have to be a geologist to appreciate the landscapes of Britain's first National Park. The 22 million day visits it receives every year show it to be one of the most popular National Parks not only in Britain, but the world, and the area it covers seems to have something for just about everybody. Visitors come to the Peak for many reasons, but for

*The courtyard of Haddon Hall, one of the most perfectly preserved medieval manor houses in England*

*Above, looking south down Dovedale from Thorpe Cloud*

*Right, Monsal Dale viaduct from Monsal Head, with Fin Cop to the left*

most it provides the chance to escape into beautiful, unspoilt countryside from the towns and cities of the north and Midlands. It is sometimes hard to believe as you look out across the wild moorland heights of Kinder or Bleaklow that just over a dozen miles (19km) in either direction, east or west, are the city centres of Manchester and Sheffield. This accessibility is at once one of the Peak's great attractions, and one of its greatest problems. The sheer number of those visitors can cause congestion in the small villages and narrow country roads, and erosion on a massive scale on some of the most popular footpaths, notably the Pennine Way which starts its 250 mile (400km) journey north at Edale.

The moors and dales of the Peak were not always as easily accessible as they are today. In the 1930s the highest and wildest moors of the Dark Peak, including Kinder and Bleaklow, were out of bounds to the rambler because they were strictly preserved grouse moors, watched over by patrolling gamekeepers. The 1932 Mass Trespass on Kinder Scout, after which five ramblers were imprisoned, saw the

start of the end of that restriction and today, thanks to access agreements negotiated by the National Park with landowners, over 80 square miles (207 sq km) have open access.

Yet bogtrotting across the moors is not everyone's cup of tea and many people prefer the gentler walking available on the 4,000 miles (6,400km) of public rights of way in the National Park. Many of these are on the limestone plateau of the White Peak, where pretty stone-built villages like Bakewell, Tideswell, Hartington, Foolow and Monyash seem to grow almost organically from the landscape. Others pass through the spectacular, crag-rimmed limestone dales of the White Peak, home of the rarest and best of the Peak's wildlife, which have been famous as visitor attractions since the 17th century.

The best known of these dales is undoubtedly Dovedale, the praises of which were first extolled by Izaak Walton and Charles Cotton in the anglers' bible, *The Compleat Angler*, first published in 1653. Walton dubbed the Dove 'the princess of rivers', and tourists have been agreeing with him ever since. But many other dales, such

as Lathkill Dale (part of the Derbyshire Dales National Nature Reserve), Bradford Dale, near Youlgreave, and the Manifold valley, just over the border in Staffordshire, are equally beautiful and often not as crowded as Dovedale, especially in high summer.

The first real tourist guide to the Peak was written by Thomas Hobbes, philosopher and tutor to the Cavendish family at Chatsworth, whose *De Mirabilibus Pecci*, or *The Wonders of the Peak*, published in 1636, became the basis for a generally accepted Grand Tour of the region. Charles Cotton of Hartington, co-author of *The Compleat Angler*, later rehashed Hobbes's seven 'wonders' in

*Autumn on Curbar Edge, looking down the Derwent valley towards Baslow Edge*

his own version, published in 1681. Nearly all these wonders were in the White Peak, and they included places like Peak Cavern, the largest cave entrance in Britain at Castleton, Poole's Cavern in Buxton, and Eldon Hole, a large open pothole near Peak Forest. Mam Tor was included because of its unstable east face which constantly sheds rocks and debris, earning it the nickname the 'Shivering Mountain', and another wonder was the palatial home of the Dukes of Devonshire at Chatsworth, newly won from the wilderness.

For many people coming from the south, the east or the Midlands, the introduction to the Peak and the Pennines is the White Peak, and the first thing that strikes these visitors from the lowland shires is the intricate system of drystone walls which spreads across the green pastures like a net. It has been estimated that, in the White Peak alone, there are 26,000 miles (41,600km) of drystone walls which, if built around the equator, would more than encircle the earth. These are mostly a legacy from the Enclosure Movements of the 18th and 19th centuries, although some have recently

been archaeologically dated to the Roman period. Certainly, early man found the Peak very much to his liking and the area is a rich treasure-house for the archaeologist and landscape historian. Almost every hilltop in this part of the Peak paradoxically carries the name low, which denotes a tumulus or burial mound, usually dating from the Bronze Age. Even earlier is the famous Neolithic stone circle, or henge, of Arbor Low, near Monyash, which has been dubbed the Stonehenge of the North. But Arbor Low's stones, unlike those of its Wiltshire contemporary, lie recumbent within a grassy embankment which has a Bronze Age barrow on its rim.

Later in the Bronze Age there seems to have been a movement towards the apparently inhospitable moors of the Dark Peak and in places like the Eastern Moor, west of Chesterfield and Sheffield, entire self-contained communities of this period have been identified. The reason for this movement is thought to have been related to a change in the climate of Britain, and weather conditions were certainly more amenable. Today, the area is only home to hawk and hare.

*Bakewell's 14th-century bridge over the River Wye leads the eye to the spire of All Saints parish church*

*The Ladybower Reservoir impounds the waters of the Upper River Derwent in the north-east of the Park*

One of the largest and highest Iron Age hillforts in the Pennines is found at Mam Tor, at the head of the broad Hope valley on the boundary between the White and Dark Peak. On this windswept, 1,695ft (517m) hill of shale and grit a sizeable population once lived, perhaps using their 'town in the sky' as a summertime shelter from which they could watch over their flocks of grazing animals. It is one of several hillforts which are scattered about the Dark Peak, usually overlooking the broad river valleys which separate it from the lush pastures of the limestone country.

The Romans came to the Peak to exploit the easily accessible veins of lead ore which criss-cross the White Peak. Their lead-mining centre, which we know from surviving pigs (ingots) of lead was called *Ludutarum*, has still not been satisfactorily identified, and the only sizeable Roman settlement which has been excavated is the small fortlet of Navio at Brough, a few miles from Mam Tor in the Hope valley, which may have been built to defend those lead-mining interests. But the heyday of the lead-mining industry in the Peak was during the 18th century when over 10,000 miners were at work in the White Peak area. The great landowners of the Peak, such as the Dukes of Devonshire at Chatsworth and the Dukes of Rutland from nearby Haddon Hall, gained much of their wealth from the mineral rights exploited by mining in the Peak and they left a legacy of rolling parkland and beautiful stately homes which adorn the valleys of the Derwent and the Wye.

The Peak has always been a dynamic, working landscape, and wherever the visitor looks he will see evidence of man's hand. The huge limestone quarries, such as those which excluded Buxton and Matlock from the boundaries of the National Park, are still very visible features from the Park, and an important source of employment for the 38,000 residents.

Even in the apparently wildest places, such as the valley of the Upper Derwent in the shadow of Bleaklow, the landscape of lake and forest is the

result of human activities. The triple reservoirs of Howden, Derwent and Ladybower were created to provide water for the growing industrial populations of the surrounding cities, and the trees were planted to protect water purity. Today, they are popular places for visitors and the subject of a traffic management scheme similar to one first introduced in the Goyt valley on the western side of the Park. Other pioneering projects by the independent National Park authority have included the transformation of derelict railway lines, such as the Tissington and High Peak Trails, into pleasant walking and riding routes. So, despite the pressures, the Peak still provides the Great Escape to the citizens of the surrounding cities.

_Thorpe Cloud, a limestone reef knoll at the southern end of Dovedale, commands fine views_

Even in its works of art, Calke Abbey breaks the mould. Rather than having the usual Print Room, as in other historic houses, the Harpurs favoured a collection of satirical caricatures on political and society themes, representing the finest exponents of the art form of their day.

# CALKE ABBEY
## *Derbyshire*

### TICKNALL, 8 MILES (13 KM) SOUTH OF DERBY

*Calke Abbey is now in the charge of the National Trust*

Calke Abbey is, perhaps, one of the few places which can rightly claim to be unique. It is certainly different from the usual stately home, and this is largely due to the family who occupied it for more than 300 years. A former Augustinian abbey was an appropriate choice of home for the Harpurs, who were noted for their reclusive tendencies. With a sizeable fortune made in Elizabethan times from the law, the Harpurs lavished a great deal of money on updating the Tudor house, first in baroque style, later in neo-classical style.

It was Sir Henry Harpur (1763-1819) who compounded the reclusive label which still attaches to his family name. He somewhat pretentiously adopted the name of the Crewe barons, distant relations by marriage, and renamed his home – but then spoilt the whole effect by marrying a lady's maid, and was ostracised by his contemporaries.

His great-grandson was another character. Sir Vauncey Harpur Crewe had an overriding passion for natural history, to the extent of hanging hunting trophies over his bed. His collection of stuffed creatures, birds' eggs, shells and walking sticks add to the eccentricities to be found around the house.

The National Trust, which acquired the property in 1985, have managed to carry out essential repairs to the house while retaining its 'time capsule' appearance.

Open April to October afternoons, except Thursday and Friday. Tel: 01332 863822.

# HARDWICK HALL
## *Derbyshire*

4½ MILES (7 KM) NORTH-WEST OF MANSFIELD

*E*lizabeth, Countess of Shrewsbury – 'Bess of Hardwick' – was a remarkable and very shrewd woman. She came from a fairly modest background and proceeded to outlive four husbands, each richer and higher on the social strata than the one that went before. With her wealth, Bess built great houses, including Chatsworth, but Hardwick Hall was the last, begun when she was 70 after the death of her fourth husband, the Earl of Shrewsbury, in 1590.

With architect Robert Smythson she created an impressive mansion with enormous windows and six great towers surmounted by her ornately fashioned monogram – ES. Inside, the Hall was designed specifically to house the collection of tapestries which still line its walls, and the Long Gallery, running the length of the east front, is hung with family portraits.

When Bess died in 1608 Hardwick passed to William Cavendish who bought his brother's share in Chatsworth and made this the principal family seat. Thus Hardwick Hall was left quite unaltered by succeeding generations.

As well as being a splendid example of its age, Hardwick has some particularly important works of embroidery, some worked by Bess herself, others by Mary, Queen of Scots, who was confined here for a time. The sumptuous embroidery of the bedhead in the state bedroom is an outstanding example.

Open from April to October on selected afternoons. Tel: 01246 850430.

*Magnificent tapestries adorn the walls of the Blue Bedroom*

*Above and right, nestling in the lovely Derwent Valley, Chatsworth is the epitome of a stately home*

# CHATSWORTH
## *Derbyshire*

1.5 MILES (2 KM) SOUTH OF BAKEWELL

In 1939 a girls' school was relocated to Chatsworth. Assemblies were held in the painted hall, physics were taught in the butler's pantry, art in the orangery, biology in the still room and chemistry out of harm's way in the stable block. There were dormitories all round the house, and 20 girls slept in the state drawing room.

This palatial home of the Dukes of Devonshire, which sits splendidly in the Derwent Valley, is one of the grandest and best-loved of all the stately homes in Britain. The first house at Chatsworth was built by Bess of Hardwick, Countess of Shrewsbury, a remarkable lady who had four husbands and grew substantially richer and more powerful with each widowhood. At Chatsworth she was with her second husband, Sir William Cavendish, and they began building here in 1552, though the development of the house continued over many years.

In 1686 the 4th Earl, who was created 1st Duke of Devonshire in 1694, began to demolish parts of it to make way for new buildings designed by Thomas Archer. He also rebuilt the west front and lived just long enough to see completed the supremely beautiful house which delights visitors today. Only the chapel, the state dining room and the sculpture gallery remained as they were originally built.

Marble statuary from the 1st century ad in the north entrance hall and the painted ceiling panel provide a hint of the glories to come, but few visitors are prepared for the breathtaking painted

hall, with the whole of the ceiling and upper walls covered with scenes from the life of Julius Caesar, painted by Louis Laguerre in 1692.

Amidst all this splendour, the children's Christmas party takes place every year, and the knowledge of this adds a delightful human touch to the beautiful but inanimate features.

The series of state rooms continues in equally grand style, suitably furnished and adorned with fine works of art and magnificent Mortlake tapestries. In the state music room there is also a touch of humour in the form of a *trompe-l'oeil* painting of a violin on an inner door which really does deceive the eye, even at very close quarters.

The bed in the state bedroom originally belonged to King George II, and on his death it was presented to the 4th Duke. King George V and Queen Mary slept here when they stayed at Chatsworth for the Royal Show at Derby in 1933.

The Oak Room is the oldest room in the house, with oak panelling and carved heads from a German monastery, one of the many purchases made by the 6th Duke. An avid collector of art and classical works, he was just one in a long line of Cavendishes who have shaped this splendid house and filled it with wonderful things.

Open from late March to October daily. Tel: 01246 582204.

# EYAM
## *Derbyshire*

### 12 MILES (19 KM) NORTH-WEST OF CHESTERFIELD

It was in one of the houses near the church, known as Plague Cottages, that in September 1665 the village tailor took delivery of a box of clothes from London that was contaminated with plague germs. The deadly disease spread rapidly through the village, the people panicked and prepared to leave. But their parson, William Mompesson, encouraged them to stay, bravely isolating the place from the outside world in order to prevent the disease spreading across the county. The heroic villagers paid dearly for their courage, for out of some 350 inhabitants, 259 died. Whole families were wiped out; the graves of one entire family, the Rileys, can be seen to the west of the village. Mompesson closed the church and held services in the open air in The Delph. His wife was one of the victims and her grave may be seen in the churchyard. Despite reminders of its sad past, Eyam (pronounced 'Eem') is none the less one of the Peak District's most pleasing villages. It has a good variety of houses built solidly, in the 17th and 18th centuries, in local gritstone and in traditional Peakland styles. Some border the square, others line the sloping main street. Beside the church is a Saxon cross, its cross-head, unusually, still intact. The ancient tradition of well-dressing is practised here.

*One of the row of six Plague Cottages, with its poignant reminder of their sad past*

The parish register for 1615 describes 'the greatest snow which ever fell uppon the Earth within man's memorye'. It lasted from January to May. Drifts covered walls and hedges and people went about 'without the sight of any earth, eyther upon hilles or valleys'. On Kinder 'uppon May day in the morning, instead of fetching in flowers, the youthes brought in flakes of snow which lay above a foot deep uppon the moores and mountaynes'. In the Peaks of Derbyshire, nature still takes the leading role.

*The village set in a limestone landscape that is patterned with the drystone walls built, stone by stone, about 200 years ago*

# YOULGREAVE
### *Derbyshire*

4 MILES (6.5 KM) SOUTH OF BAKEWELL

*E*xplore Derbyshire in the summer months and you are likely to come across the ancient art of well-dressing. It is not just wells that are dressed nowadays. In Youlgreave the public taps are adorned with these elaborate pictures made of flowers, mosses, seeds and cones, as well as its fountain. This is an attractive old lead-mining village high up in limestone Peakland. Its main street straggles along the hillside above the River Bradford, dominated by the big battlemented, pinnacled and gargoyled tower of the Norman church, one of the best in the area. Inside, it is all sturdy columns and capitals. The 13th-century font uniquely has two bowls, and there is a panel of similar date showing a Norman in a long robe. The excellent monuments include an effigy of Thomas Cokayne (*d.*1488) remarkable for its tiny size. The church was restored in 1870 by Norman Shaw and has stained-glass windows by Burne-Jones and Kempe. There are some good 18th-century stone houses near by, and to the west are Old Hall Farm (1630) and Old Hall (1650), both lovely hall houses. The area is rich in prehistory and 2 miles (3km) west of the village is Arbor Low, an Early Bronze Age stone circle, similar to but smaller than Stonehenge and Avebury. Its stones lie flat, in a circle about 250ft (76m) in diameter.

# KEDLESTON HALL
## *Derbyshire*

### 5 MILES (8 KM) NORTH-WEST OF DERBY

Sir Nathanial Curzon had a passion for naval affairs and frequently conducted mock battles on the lake, with frigates manned by estate workers.

*Kedleston was the home of the Curzons for over 800 years*

*M*any grand mansions claim to be the finest example of the work of the brilliant Scottish architect, Robert Adam, but Kedleston Hall is well up in the running. Its planning began, however, as something of a muddle. Sir Nathanial Curzon, who inherited the estate in 1758, accepted a design submitted by Matthew Brettingham and James Paine, and they had already built the pavilions and started on the ground floor of the main house when, in December 1758, Curzon was introduced to Robert Adam. He was so impressed by Adam's ideas that he gave him the job of directing the work of Kedleston Hall.

The entrance front has been described as the grandest Palladian façade in Britain; at its centre there is a vast Corinthian portico set on a high base with flights of steps on either side.

The interiors are no less impressive, and the first introduction is the magnificent Marble Hall, modelled on the ancient atrium of the classic Roman villa. The drawing room has a nautical theme, from the decorative plaster ceiling of grotesque sea creatures to the gilt settees carved with mermaids, tritons and dolphins. All around the house are fine works of art, including Old Masters, family portraits and superb furniture.

The Indian Museum displays the collection of one Lord Curzon's time as Viceroy of India.

Open from April to October daily, except Monday and Tuesday, but open for Bank Holiday Mondays. Tel: 01332 842191.

# CROMFORD
## *Derbyshire*

2 MILES (3 KM) SOUTH OF MATLOCK

*The Arkwright Society is involved in major restoration work on this, the first cotton mill in the country*

This is Richard Arkwright's village, and the place where the factory system was born at the beginning of the Industrial Revolution. Once he had invented the spinning machine, Arkwright went on to build England's first cotton mill, in 1771, in the beautiful Derwent valley. The huge mill building still stands, close to a medieval bridge over the river whose waters Arkwright chose to power his machines. His wharves and storage buildings are ranged beside the canal that was constructed in 1793 to link his mill with the major cities of the North and the Midlands. He also built cottages to house his workers, the best examples being in North Street

– austere terraces of solid, three-storeyed gritstone houses, the top floors of which were probably used as workshops. Smaller cottages, also gritstone, climb Cromford Hill away from the river. In the centre of the village he built The Greyhound Inn. Near the bridge is the church he built in 1797. It was gothicised by the Victorians. He also provided chapels and a Sunday school, creating a complete new village for the workforce in what had been until then an unpopulated location. On the other side of the Derwent, in proud position to admire his works, is his own house, Willersley Castle, which sadly he did not see completed before he died in 1792.

The dawning of the Industrial Revolution was seen by contemporaries to exemplify man's triumphs over nature, and these early feats were often the subject of painting or poetry. Erasmus Darwin wrote of Cromford, 'where Derwent guides his dusky floods/ Through vaulted mountains and a night of woods', inspired not only by the picturesque situation of Arkwright's first mill but also by the industrial architecture and the innovative machinery it housed. It is only with our hindsight that we see countryside devastated in the name of progress.

# MIDLAND RAILWAY CENTRE
*Derbyshire*

RIPLEY, 10 MILES (16 KM) NORTH OF DERBY

*In 1994 the Midland Railway celebrated its 150th anniversary*

*T*he Midland Railway Trust is not just for railway buffs, though it does have an excellent working line of 3½ miles (5km) with three stations along the way. One of these stations also has a large museum, a farm park with lots of animals, a country park and a narrow gauge railway. Tourist railways are increasingly trying to expand their range of activities or points of interest to broaden their appeal and in this respect the Midland Railway Centre has succeeded admirably. The centre was something of a pioneer, starting off with a grandiose vision, and this was, in part, because it was the brainchild of local authorities who wanted to commemorate the railway which had had such an impact on the county town and its environs. Credit for the realisation of this bold plan, however, is due to the volunteer organisation formed to support the venture, since local government reorganisation ended the role of local authorities as the driving force.

The line itself is the remains of a

Midland Railway branch that was built primarily for coal and goods traffic but also had a suburban service from Derby. At Hammersmith, the western terminus of the Centre, a line went off west to Ambergate. Its survival was largely due to the rail connection to the famous Butterley Company ironworks, set up in the 1790s – its most famous contract was the roof for St Pancras station in London, but it also exported widely, and iron-work for such stations as Buenos Aires was taken out by the Midland

Railway for transfer to the docks.

A journey over this line begins at Butterley. There was nothing left of the original structures so the handsome station building was moved stone by stone from Whitwell in the north of the county. A model railway, buffet and shop help to pass the time before departure for Swanwick and Riddings Junction. The signal box at Butterley, one of four Midland Railway boxes on the line, was originally at the remote site of Ais Gill on the Settle & Carlisle railway.

*Signal-changing: the railway has three working restored signal boxes and a fourth on display at the museum*

The Centre's museum (best visited on the return journey from Riddicks Junction) is passed on the right as the train steams past Swanwick Junction. As the valley opens up, cottages beside the Cromford Canal can be seen, and on a hillside to the south is a monument to William Jessop, who both built the canal and helped to found the Butterley Company. At Riddick Junction the locomotive runs round the train before returning to Swanwick; in due course the line will be extended to a new station beside the Nottingham–Sheffield line.

The complex at Swanwick could take much of the day to see properly. It is dominated by the Matthew Kirtley Museum, named after a locomotive superintendent of the Midland who designed one of the locomotives in the museum. This huge building contains most of the Centre's stock and also functions as a repair shop for both steam and diesel engines. Behind the shed is an engineering workshop, to which access is limited, and beyond that a miniature railway. A road transport museum is under construction for the display of a collection ranging from early bicycles to double-decker buses. Past Johnson's Buffet (named after another Midland Railway locomotive superintendent) is Brittain Pit Farm Park, centred on a range of brick buildings, where a wide variety of animals can be seen at close quarters. Near the demonstration signal box, in which a signalman illustrates the intricacies of the job, a narrow gauge railway takes visitors into the 35-acre (14ha) country park. Here a network of paths leads to a series of ponds, to the remains of Grumblethorpe Colliery and to the mouth of the Cromford Canal tunnel. This was blocked off in 1909 following an earlier collapse through subsidence. The canal was finally abandoned in 1944, although recent restoration of the Ambergate–Cromford section has returned boats to that part of the waterway.

An alternative to taking the train back from Swanwick Junction is to walk along the top of the cutting between there and Butterley. However, westbound trains run through Butterley without stopping, so if you plan to do this, make sure you purchase a ticket for unlimited travel, which applies on all but a few special days. Then you can catch an outward train again, and return the whole way by rail.

The last section of the line is one of the most photographed, crossing a long stone embankment across Butterley Reservoir; this structure was built in the 1930s to replace a bridge. At Hammersmith, the locomotive again runs round, under the control of a signal box rescued from Kilby Bridge, Leicester. Work is in progress here to create a small country station.

Train service: on 214 days during the year. Tel: 01773 570140.

*Right: getting ready for the off in traditional manner*

*Opposite: BR 2-6-4T No 80080, one of the 15 locomotives currently in service on the line*

# HADDON HALL
## *Derbyshire*

### 2 MILES (3 KM) SOUTH-EAST OF BAKEWELL

Perched high above the River Wye on a limestone escarpment, Haddon Hall is one of the most romantic medieval castles in England. The grey and honey colour of its stonework is a sharp contrast to the rich green of the woodland behind, and beautiful gardens spill down in a series of walled terraces from Dorothy Vernon's door at the very top of the bowling alley. When the 9th Duke of Rutland restored Haddon in 1912, he cleared this terrace of giant yews, as well as sycamores and ivy on the walls. Pairs of clipped yew trees are again a feature of this garden which, in the spring, glows with more than 60 varieties of daffodils, polyanthus and wallflowers. As summer approaches, the roses take

*The fountain terrace, with its beds of roses and lavender, and the Elizabethan border below the gallery windows*

castle almost to the level of the river itself. Tradition has it that Haddon came into the hands of the Dukes of Rutland when the Vernon heiress eloped with John Manners, son of the then Earl of Rutland, in the 1560s, running down the 76 drystone steps and across the packhorse bridge to meet her lover.

Whatever the truth of the story, the steps from Dorothy Vernon's door, which is the route by which the modern visitor leaves the house, descend to a terrace which was once a

over: first the climbers, including *Rosa primula*, the incense rose, and then the floribundas and the hybrid teas in the formal beds. Haddon also boasts a collection of clematis, with 'Mrs Cholmondley' showing large, blue blooms in early summer beside the upper door.

A wide flight of steps leads down to the Fountain Terrace which lies beneath the irregular window panes of the magnificent Jacobean long gallery. A simple, rectangular pool with its delicate jet of water contrasts with the

surrounding lawn and the beds that show favourites such as 'King's Ransom' and 'Wendy Cussons', while the gallery wall itself is covered with a variety of climbing roses coloured pink, yellow and deep red. Beneath this magnificent display is an Elizabethan border, with native plants and those introduced during the 16th century – aquilegias, dame's violet and love-lies-bleeding, while, further along, is a bed with more than 30 varieties of delphiniums that make a splendid display in early July.

From the end of Fountain Terrace there are spectacular views over the Wye and the surrounding countryside. Although the lower terraces are not open to the public, the retaining walls harbour a wide range of rock plants which create a colourful patchwork during the spring, raising the question of whether the medieval lords of Haddon planted a series of gardens in these defensive terraces the equal of those we so admire today.

Open from Easter to September, on selected days. Tel: 01629 812855.

*Part of the display of over 30 varieties of delphiniums*

*Sheep graze peacefully below Beeby's Tub*

# BEEBY
## *Leicestershire*

### 5 MILES (8 KM) NORTH-EAST OF LEICESTER

*In summer's heat and winter's cold*
*One constant temperature I hold.*
*When brooks and wells and rivers dry*
*I always yield a full supply.*
*My neighbours say (I'm often told)*
*I'm more than worth my weight in gold.*
(Inscription in stone on the village well)

'Beeby's Tub' is unlikely nomenclature for a church spire. It certainly suggests there may be a story to tell. And, indeed, there are several legends attached to this stump of a spire that squats unfinished on the handsome ironstone tower of All Saints' Church, Beeby. One explanation is that the builder felt he could never compete with the highly decorative spire of nearby Queniborough Church, and threw himself off in despair. Another story is that the builders were brothers who had a quarrel up there. One pushed the other to his death from the battlements, and then felt such remorse that he too jumped, following his brother to his grave.

Or maybe the money just ran out. This rather fine church is no longer used for services but is being maintained by the Redundant Churches' Fund. Near it the Victorians erected a cover over the well that would have been the villagers' water supply for many centuries. Certainly there is evidence of a pre-Norman village which was deserted in the Middle Ages. The church stands beside a field, cut by a stream and shaded by an old Wellingtonia. Also here are The Manor House, The Grange, an old, beautifully restored yeoman farmhouse and some brick cottages which once housed a brewery. Stray hops still grow in the hedges of this tiny, peaceful place.

# ASHBY DE LA ZOUCH
*Leicestershire*

ASHBY-DE-LA-ZOUCH, 9 MILES (14.5 KM) SOUTH-EAST OF
BURTON UPON TRENT

*The impressive ruins of Ashby de la Zouch include the splendid 15th-century Warwick Tower*

*A*hall was founded at Ashby in the 12th century, but its principal feature, the keep, was not built until the 15th century. The owner, William, Lord Hastings, was granted a licence to convert the hall into a castle in 1474, at the same time as he started building his picturesque fortified house at Kirby Muxloe. Hastings' keep was about 90 feet (27m) tall and had four floors. There was also an extension on the north-east side of the tower, which had seven floors. Although there were already two wells in the castle, the keep had another of its own – a sensible precaution, for it meant that no one could tamper with the water supply.

Lord Hastings' own story shows how fortunes and the favour of kings could rise and fall in the Middle Ages. He rose to power dramatically under the Yorkist King Edward IV, becoming Lord Chamberlain as a reward for his loyalty throughout the Wars of the Roses. After Edward's death in 1483, Hastings, on the advice of Edward's mistress Jane Shore, refused to support his successor, Richard III. Richard had Hastings beheaded – a scene in history that was immortalised in Shakespeare's *Richard III*.

Open daily from April to October. Tel: 01530 413343.

# GREAT CENTRAL RAILWAY
## *Leicestershire*

### LOUGHBOROUGH, 9 MILES (14.5 KM) NORTH OF LEICESTER

With so many preserved railways in Britain, it is difficult to offer visitors something unique, but the Great Central Railway succeeds as the only line to re-create the atmosphere of the main line railway complete with double track and goods loops for expresses to overtake slower trains. The line is well placed to do this, since the route was once part of Britain's last great main line, the Great Central Railway, which ran from just north of Nottingham to a new London terminus at Marylebone. It was intended by its visionary chairman, Sir Edward Watkin, to become part of a continuous railway from the north of England to France, through a tunnel under the English Channel which was to be built

*Loughborough station, the largest in preservation*

by an associated company. Today's Great Central serves as a reminder of that superbly engineered line, most of which was closed during the 1960s.

The starting point for most passengers is Loughborough, where the station is the largest in preservation. Film companies often take advantage of its size, emphasised by the long, ornate canopy along the island platform; the station was recently used for the filming of *Shadowlands*, starring Anthony Hopkins. Before boarding a train, passengers are invited to inspect the impressive workshops and engine shed, which can be reached by a footpath to the north of the station. The original signal box that still controls train movements at the station stands beside the path, and visitors are normally welcomed by the signalman. There is also a museum in part of the old lift shaft for luggage, which gives visitors a good idea of the history of the railway on which they are about to travel.

As befits a main line railway, the Great Central has some large steam locomotives amongst its fleet of 23, and it frequently has visiting engines to add variety. Leaving Loughborough for the half-hour journey, you are soon in lovely countryside, often with woods on the horizon as a backdrop to the gently undulating landscape.

The first station, at Quorn & Woodhouse, has a picnic site adjacent to the typical island platform

*Stoking the firebox*

arrangment, in which tracks pass either side of a single platform. Shortly beyond Quorn is the scenic highlight of the journey as the train crosses Swithland Reservoir on a long viaduct. Now a sanctuary for birds, the reservoir had to be drained for the construction of the viaduct. At Swithland Sidings the Great Central Railway's impressive work to restore the look of the old main line can be best appreciated, though there is no station here. The goods loops have been installed here and double-tracking south to Rothley is underway. You may also see a goods train of seemingly endless coal wagons pass by, for another Great Central project is

*Watering time again*

there-creation of the 'Windcutter' fast coal trains which once used the line. To achieve this, a large number of 16-ton mineral wagons has been assembled.

Try to find time to break your journey at Rothley, for it is a delightful station with one of the best preserved rooms – the humble, but superbly refurbished parcels office. The station is gaslit and has been restored using the colours of the old Great Central Railway. The signal box was rescued from Wembley in London to replace the original, long since demolished; its most notorious inhabitant was a signalman with a penchant for nude bathing in the station watertrough. The large shed to the east of the line is the railway's carriage shed and works.

Leaving Rothley, look out for Rothley Brook which was used as a canal in Roman times. Just beyond the site of Belgrave & Birstall station, demolished in 1977, is the Great Central's new southern terminus. This promises to be one of the most ambitious ever projects in railway preservation, for the intention is to build a three-platform station with a two-storey building based on Marylebone. A new engine shed, turntable and museum will be provided, with events lawn and adjacent nature reserve.

One day the Great Central may operate trains to the outskirts of Nottingham, for at the country park at Ruddington an affiliated group is creating a northern base from which it is hoped to lay track to the south. This would double the present run of 7½ miles (12km).

Train service: weekends all year, weekdays from May to September. Santa specials. Tel: 01509 230726.

*London & North East Railway's No 1306, the Mayflower*

# NEWSTEAD ABBEY
## *Nottinghamshire*

LINBY

*A*lthough associated with the name of the poet, Lord Byron, Newstead Abbey has a long and distinguished history in which its gardens play an appropriately important part. Founded by Henry II as a priory in the 12th century, Newstead was acquired by Sir John Byron of Colwick at the dissolution of the monasteries, and the 5th Lord Byron, as well as being tried for murder and acquitted, was responsible for adding the Upper Lake to the 25 acres (10ha) of gardens, which came into the hands of Nottinghamshire County Council on presentation by the last owner, Sir Julian Caln, in the 1930s.

From the entry to the 300 acre (120ha) estate alongside the so-called Gospel Oak, the long drive sweeps through rhododendron plantations that date from the last century, and crosses open heathland covered with heather to reach a car park to the north of the abbey. Water flows over a cascade into the Garden Lake, and the walls of the house are festooned with jasmine and the fragrant yellow rose 'Golden Showers'. Close to the east wall is the Spanish Garden, named after an Iberian well-head which is its centrepiece. This gives on to a gravel path bounded by a wall covered with hydrangeas and honeysuckles, its border filled with shade-loving plants. A pocket handkerchief tree marks the entry to a dark, dank tunnel which leads to Eagle Pond, one of the monks' original stew ponds. Just to the west is the famous memorial to Boatswain, Byron's dog, and the wood

*Swathes of roses, ancient and modern, adorn the former kitchen garden*

*A colourful border with shades graduating from blues and pinks to warm reds and gold*

beyond is planted with snowdrops and daffodils which make a brave show in spring.

In the former kitchen garden beds at each end display old-fashioned roses, while modern roses are set in beds surrounded by lawns, and climbers and ramblers adorn the walls of the enclosure. Beyond the great Yew Walk is a fine rock garden and also the famous Japanese Garden commissioned by Miss Ethel Webb, whose family owned Newstead in the early years of this century. Hump-backed bridges and stepping stones across the streams lead between rhododendrons, azaleas, mahonias, skimmias and bamboo. Returning to the Garden Lake, you can enjoy the beauty of a pergola covered with roses and other climbers, and what is probably the best view of the abbey in this extensive and beautiful garden.

Open daily. Tel: 01623 793557.

*Bridges and stepping stones show the way through the famous Japanese Garden*

*One of the old stone cottages grouped contentedly together in the heart of the village*

# AYNHO
## *Northamptonshire*

### 6 MILES (9.5 KM) SOUTH-EAST OF BANBURY

There is a story that in 1646 Robert Wylde applied for the post of rector here. He and the other applicant were required to preach a sermon, after which a vote was taken. When asked the result, Wylde is said to have replied that it was divided: ' I got the Ay, he the No.'

River, canal, railway and now motorway twist their way like plaited ribbons along the Cherwell valley below this hilly, limestone village. It is a village on a main (A41) road, but has some enticing and rewarding nooks and crannies to explore. The church dates from the 14th century and there may even have been a settlement here before the Normans, but most of the notable buildings in the village date from the 17th century onwards, when the Cartwright family bought the manor here. It is said that they used to claim the rent from their tenants in the form of apricots, and to this day a number of apricot trees can be seen growing on sunny house fronts. Apricots like the local limestone soil. During the Civil War, in 1645, Royalist troops burnt the Cartwrights' house down, but they had it rebuilt, and at about the same time the church too was rebuilt to match it. It is symmetrical, two-storeyed, and looks like a grand house. The old grammar school is a fine building, dated to 1671, and near by are the two-storeyed almshouses built in 1822. There are lovely grey-gold limestone houses and cottages everywhere. Opposite the old coaching inn, The Cartwright Arms, by the green, is the village hall built with stone from the medieval pesthouse where plague victims were isolated.

# SULGRAVE MANOR
## *Northamptonshire*

### 6 MILES (9.5 KM) NORTH-EAST OF BANBURY

*I*n 1914, just as the Great War was beginning, Sulgrave Manor was set up as a memorial to mark 100 years of peace between Britain and America. Sulgrave was the obvious choice – the ancestral home of George Washington, the first President of the United States of America. It was also in need of restoration, and funds were raised on both sides of the Atlantic to finance the operation. Many items relating to George Washington are now on display in the house, including his velvet coat, saddle bags, a lock of his hair, various documents and portraits.

One of the most interesting aspects of the exterior of the house is the Washington coat of arms above the main porch, its motif of mullets (stars) and bars (stripes) not surprisingly held to be the inspiration for the American Flag.

The first Washington to live here was Lawrence, Mayor of Northampton, who purchased the manor in 1539. It was his grandson, John, who emigrated to Virginia and became the great-grandfather of the first President.

George Washington memorabilia aside, Sulgrave is a fascinating house to visit, with some wonderful old pieces of furniture, and is all the more charming for its modest proportions.

Open from April to October daily, except Wednesday; March, November and December, weekends only. Tel: 01295 760205.

*The Washington family arms above the front door may have inspired the design of the American flag*

During the restoration of the Great Hall a silver sixpence dated 1568, an Elizabethan baby's shoe and a decorated knife case (thought to have belonged to Lawrence Washington) were discovered in a crevice between the ceiling and the floor above.

# COTTESBROOKE HALL
## *Northamptonshire*

COTTESBROOKE, 9 MILES (14.5 KM) NORTH-WEST OF NORTHAMPTON

To the north of Northampton, in that secluded countryside which saw the Civil War battle of Naseby, is the early 18th-century Cottesbrooke Hall. Thought to be the model used by Jane Austen for *Mansfield Park*, the lovely house and its surrounding gardens are approached over the classical Mitchell Bridge. The splendid parkland was also created at the same time, but by an unknown hand, and the more formal layout and the Wild Garden were devised by Edward Schultz, Sir Geoffrey Jellicoe and Dame Sylvia Crowe, though inspired by the late Hon. Lady Macdonald-Buchanan. The result is a series of charming enclosed courtyards and gardens around the house, immaculately maintained by the present owners, Captain and Mrs J Macdonald-Buchanan, and their head gardener, Mrs Daw.

On entering the garden opposite the west wing, there is a magnificent view of the lake and of Brixworth Church,

*Great cedars of Lebanon offer shelter to the borders on the terrace*

which dates originally from Anglo Saxon times. A large tulip tree, an *Acer griseum* and several magnolias can be seen, while the forecourt to the garden in front of the house has large vases planted with rhododendrons and agapanthus. Beyond the wrought-iron gates and two rose beds is the Statue Walk, with Peter Scheemakers's four statues from the Temple of Ancient Virtue, at Stowe, backed by clipped yews and facing a herbaceous border, while on either side of Eagle Gates are further borders with large wisterias and a fragrant pineapple-scented Moroccan broom. To the east is the Dilemma Garden with, between its 'horns', old roses, a fastigiate tulip tree, a golden Indian bean, a pocket handkerchief tree and an old mulberry. Opposite is the Pool Garden with some fine magnolias, a large

*Carpentaria californica* with its glossy dark green foliage, ceanothus and a lovely *Actinidia kolomikta*.

*An overflowing urn stands before the pergola*

In the Dutch Garden, with its two sundials, there is spectacular spring and summer bedding within miniature box hedges, while the Pine Court alongside is dominated by an old Scots pine with a climbing hydrangea. The terrace has extensive herbaceous borders with a wonderful display of foliage plants, including yuccas and euphorbias, partly sheltered by ancient cedars of Lebanon.

In early May the Spinney Garden shines with brightly coloured bulbs and azaleas, a snakebark maple, a Tibetan cherry, a Judas tree, and weeping beeches. Beyond a thatched Wendy house, a small stream flows beside two wild gardens planted with azaleas, rhododendrons, primroses and daffodils. Hostas, hellebores, ligularias and astilbes grow in profusion by the bridge, and there is also a bank of bamboos in front of the so-called Japanese yew.

Open from April to September, on one afternoon a week and some bank holidays. Tel: 01604 505732.

# TATTERSHALL CASTLE
## *Lincolnshire*

### 8 MILES (13 KM) SOUTH-WEST OF HORNCASTLE

Surrounded by a moat and earthworks, the great red-brick tower of Tattershall stands proudly in the rolling Lincolnshire countryside. The tower is vast, its red-brown brick contrasting vividly with the bright white stone of its windows and 'machicolations' – projecting parapets with holes in them to permit objects to be thrown or fired at attackers.

Records show that nearly one million bricks were used to build the 100 foot (30m) high tower and associated buildings. It was constructed between 1430 and 1450 for Ralph, Lord Cromwell, who was Treasurer of England. Cromwell wanted Tattershall to be an aggressive statement of his power and authority, hence the formidable array of machicolations 80 feet (24m) above the ground, and the once extensive systems of water-filled moats and earthworks.

Like many barons of his day, Cromwell wanted his home comforts as well as security, and inside the tower are six floors of fine chambers, each with small rooms in the corner towers. Visitors may well have the curious feeling that the rooms are getting larger as they head upwards, and this is actually the case – it was not necessary to have such thick walls in the upper floors, which were less likely to be attacked than the lower ones.

Open from April to October, daily except Monday and Tuesday. Tel: 01526 342543.

*Lord Curzon, Viceroy of India, bought and restored Tattershall, presenting it to the National Trust in 1925*

*Lincoln Castle is a popular spot for 'living history' events*

# LINCOLN CASTLE
## Lincolnshire

LINCOLN, 16 MILES (26 KM) NORTH-EAST OF NEWARK-ON-TRENT

*I*n 1068 William the Conqueror ordered that a castle should be built in Lincoln on a site that had been occupied since Roman times, and 166 houses were cleared away in order to make room for it. It seems inconceivable today that so many people could be uprooted from their homes at a moment's notice, but such cavalier actions on the part of landowners were not uncommon in medieval times, and the historical records of many castles tell of such clearances.

Lincoln is one of the very few castles in Britain that has two 'mottes' or castle mounds (Lewes in East Sussex is another). The larger of these two mottes has a 15-sided keep called the Lucy Tower, named after the mother of a 12th-century owner, Lucy, Countess of Chester. The smaller motte has a square tower with a 19th-century observatory, and huge 12th-century walls join the two mottes and enclose an area of about five acres (2ha).

Until recently, Lincoln housed a prison, and one of the most interesting features is the prison chapel, designed as a series of small cubicles so that the prisoners could not see each other.

Open all year daily, except Sundays and Christmas Day. Tel: 01522 511068.

# DODDINGTON HALL
## *Lincolnshire*

### 3 MILES (5 KM) SOUTH OF LINCOLN

*Below and right, from the outside Doddington Hall betrays its Elizabethan pedigree, but inside, 18th-century elegance prevails*

D oddington House has the distinction of never having been sold, but it has passed by marriage through four families – the Tailors, the Husseys, the Delavels and finally the Jarvises, who are the present occupants. It was originally built for Thomas Tailor by the Elizabethan architect, Robert Smithson.

The white hall, which was the Great Hall in Elizabethan times, is still used on special occasions as a dining room; it is overlooked by portraits of ancestors of the Hussey and Delavel families. Rare gilt *carton pierre* ornaments and gilt mirror frames, bought by John Delavel in 1775, adorn the drawing room, a staggering 52ft (15.8m) in length, which appears today just as it did in the 18th century. In Elizabethan times the Long Gallery had windows along both sides and was used by the family for exercise and recreation. According to records, in 1756 that exercise would have included its use as a bowling alley!

More stately pleasures ensued in the 1760s when John Delavel turned it into a picture gallery. His interest in art may well have been fuelled by the family friendship with Sir Joshua Reynolds, who painted the full-length portrait of Sir Francis Delavel which hangs at the foot of the front stairs; they were an artistic family in any case – two small paintings of Seaton Delavel, the principal family home of the Delavels, painted by Edward

Hussey Delavel, may be seen above a cabinet at the top of the stairs.

The artistic bent continued into the Jarvis family, and the Print Room commemorates the life and work of George Ralph Payne Jarvis, the first member of his family to live at Doddington and a man of many talents. A solicitor by profession, he was also an accomplished artist and woodcarver, as examples of his work on display at Doddington show.

In the Tiger Room is a magnificent four-poster bed with crimson hangings of Spitalfields silk, which had to be transported to Doddington Hall by sea. The walls are hung with beautiful Flemish tapestries brought here from other rooms around the house. Several portraits, including one of Thomas Tailor, the son of the builder of Doddington Hall, decorate the oak panelled walls of the parlour, preserved in its original Queen Anne style.

Extensive parkland surrounds the Hall and there is a delightful walled rose garden.

Open from May to September on selected days. Tel: 01522 694308.

North of Grantham and close to the busy A1 lies the secluded oasis of Marston Hall. A number of small gardens and courtyards flanked by walls and high hedges surround the ancient house built of Ancaster stone, creating a setting which is at once wholly consistent with and redolent of the medieval period in which Marston Hall was originally built. Although today owned by the Reverend Henry Thorold, a cousin of the 15th baronet, Sir Anthony Thorold, Marston Hall used to be the principal seat of one of the oldest families in Lincolnshire.

From the drive up to the 3 acre (1ha) garden you can see one of the largest wych elms in the country standing opposite the main door of the house. Approximately 12ft (3.5m) in diameter, it is perhaps 400 years old, and, in spite of having been attacked by Dutch elm disease, it is now putting out new shoots. Just as remarkable is the great laburnum, in the Shrubbery Walk, close to the entrance to the churchyard, which is thought to be one of the largest in England and was planted in the late 16th century.

To the south of the house is a splendid rose garden, enclosed by yew hedges, and with climbers draped on wooden pyramids in the traditional manner, and old-fashioned roses as well as modern varieties planted in formal beds. Beyond this is a secluded area, with hedges surrounding herbaceous borders and vegetables, and a Gothick gazebo decorated with murals by Barbara Jones. A knot garden is filled with herbs, among them rosemary, thyme and mints, and beyond the lawns there are romantic walks through the newly planted Laburnum Avenue.

To mark the Reverend Thorold's retirement from the staff of Lancing College, the Lancing Avenue of Lombardy poplars has been planted. It stretches from the orchard westward to the River Witham near by, achieving a perfect synthesis between the formal layout of the garden and the parkland beyond. In every respect, Marston Hall evokes the history of this part of Lincolnshire and of the families that have lived there for many centuries.

Open on selected afternoons and by appointment.

# MARSTON HALL
## *Lincolnshire*

MARSTON, 6 MILES (9.5 KM) NORTH OF GRANTHAM

*Above, pyramids of wooden trellis stand in the rose garden, an elegant architectural feature in their own right*

*Left, a tranquil corner*

# SKEGNESS
## *Lincolnshire*

19 MILES (31 KM) NORTH OF BOSTON

### Long-Lived Old Salt

Skegness's famous symbol of the Jolly Fisherman, with his boots and heavy jersey, pipe clutched firmly in mouth, arms outspread and scarf blowing in the breeze, came from a painting by an artist named John Hassall, which the Great Northern Railway bought for £12 in 1908. That would be well over £500 today, but it was still a good investment. The Fisherman has been promoting Skegness ever since, and there are two statues of him in the town.

*Bright and breezy: a helter-skelter and a carousel wait for the day to start at Skegness*

'Skegness is SO Bracing', the railway posters used to say. The former fishing village was turned into a seaside resort by the local landowner, the ninth Earl of Scarborough, who in the 1870s succeeded in persuading the Great Northern Railway to run its line on from Wainfleet to the coast. The new resort's broad, tree-lined streets and gardens, while 25,000 coloured light bulbs glitter along the front at night. Funfair rides, TV-personality entertainment, discos, boating lakes and a model village add to the fun, and the country's first Butlin's holiday camp has been transformed into the huge Funcoast World leisure and water park. There is stock car racing at Skegness Stadium, and pleasure flights

*Carousel horses of blinding opulence, at rest in a Skegness funfair*

comfortable Victorian villas were planned to attract middle-class customers, but in fact the railway brought holidaymakers in thousands from the Midlands industrial towns. Today Skegness's miles of golden sand are backed by acres of flower-packed from the aerodrome. The Natureland zoo, with its giant aquarium, rescues orphaned seal pups. Church Farm Museum evokes life on a typical small farm at the turn of the century. To the south are the dunes and salt-marshes of the Gibraltar Point nature reserve.

# BOSTON
## *Lincolnshire*

### 28 MILES (45 KM) SOUTH-EAST OF LINCOLN

Visible for miles around across the flat fen country is the oddly nicknamed Boston Stump, the majestic and far from stumpy tower of St Botolph's Church. Rising 272 feet (83m) high and crowned with a beautiful octagonal lantern, it commands sweeping views, as far as Lincoln in clear weather. Attached to it is one of England's largest parish churches, dating from the 14th century and a splendid testimony to the town's wealth in the Middle Ages as a port exporting wool and cloth to the Netherlands. Inside the church are misericords carved with grotesque scenes, brasses, effigies and monuments. The south-west chapel was restored in 1857 by the citizens of Boston, Massachusetts, in memory of John Cotton, a former vicar here who became a leading 17th-century Puritan divine in America. The attractive town stands on the River Witham, a little way inland from the Wash. The river had silted up badly by the 16th century, but was cleared again by 18th-century improvements. The busiest port in this part of Lincolnshire, it is also the market town of a rich farming region. The 18th-century Corporation Buildings and the later Assembly Rooms dignify the market place. In the Guildhall stand the cells in which the original Pilgrim Fathers were incarcerated in 1607.

St Botolph's Town!
*Far over leagues of land
And leagues of sea looks forth
  its noble tower,
And far around the chiming
  bells are heard:
So may that sacred name for
  ever stand
A landmark, and a symbol of
  the power
That lies concentrated in a
  single word.*
Longfellow, *Boston* (1876)

*Serene above the Witham, Boston Stump has been a landmark for travellers, sailors and aviators for centuries*

# ELTON HALL
## *Cambridgeshire*

### 8 MILES (13 KM) WEST OF PETERBOROUGH

Just to the west of Peterborough, in the gently undulating countryside that stretches towards Oundle and Rockingham Forest, is the fine estate of Elton Hall. There has been a house on the site since the Norman Conquest, and the family of the present owners, Mr and Mrs William Proby, have lived there for 300 years. Such continuity is apparent not only in

*Perfect blooms in the rose garden*

'rooms' and to provide a magnificent backdrop to the knot herb garden and statuary. The Victorian Rose Garden is now a delight, not least because of the scent of the 1000 roses that drifts upwards on a still, hot day in July, and because of the interest of the many old-fashioned varieties that can be seen. 'Mutabilis' stands alongside the white and blush-pink flowers of the

the building itself, which, though constructed in the main from the 17th century, incorporates the Sapcote Tower and a chapel, both dating from about 1485, but also in the gardens, which were laid out between 1909 and 1911. When Mr and Mrs Proby came to Elton in 1979 the gardens were in a very poor state, and a programme of clearance had to be undertaken before restoration could begin. It is a tribute to their determination and plantsmanship that the gardens now provide a worthy setting for such a splendid house.

In order to re-establish the bones of the Edwardian layout hedges have been planted mainly in yew and in hornbeam to separate the different upright Bourbon, 'Boule de Neige', while 'Gruss en Aachen', *Rosa mundi* and 'Sander's White Rambler' can also be seen.

In the middle of the lovely Sunken Garden there is a lily pond, and the borders are bright in summer with an unusual selection of foliage and flowering plants, among them *Papaver orientale* 'Mrs Perry', peonies, *Philadelphus* 'Manteau d'Hermine' with its fragrant creamy-white flowers, and with *Crambe cordifolia*. The Shrub Garden shows *Viburnum opulus* 'Compactum' with its profuse white flowers, smooth sumach, the bottlebrush buckeye underplanted with hostas, and *Hydrangea arborescens*, while the herbaceous border below the Sapcote Tower is about to be replanted with a blue and yellow colour scheme. The deep border along the terrace now has pink and silver plants, and includes some roses, while clematis climbs up the walls.

A recent project has been the planting of an arboretum which includes *Keaki zelkova serrata*, evergreen oak, *Paulownia tomentosa*, the foxglove tree, the dawn redwood and *Fagus sylvatica* 'Dawyck Purple', which has erect branches. The restoration of this 8 acre (3ha) garden is a welcome initiative, that will appeal both to the plant lover and to those who just appreciate a beautiful setting.

Open from Easter to August, on selected afternoons.

*A profusion of old-fashioned roses in red, white and all shades of pink*

Queen Victoria stayed at Wimpole in 1843 and this event is now commemorated annually by school children donning the costumes of servants and preparing for the royal visit.

# WIMPOLE HALL
## *Cambridgeshire*

### 6 MILES (9.5 KM) NORTH OF ROYSTON

*The splendid proportions of Wimpole Hall, below and right, owe their origin to a number of famous architects through the ages*

The largest house in the county, Wimpole Hall is interesting on several counts. It was begun in the 17th century and continued to develop over the years – unremarkable in itself, for many houses followed this course, but it is the number of important architects who had a hand in that development which distinguishes Wimpole.

James Gibbs was responsible for the wonderfully elegant painted library built to house the famous Harley collection of 50,000 books, 40,000 prints and 300,000 pamphlets – all sold to meet financial demands made on the 2nd Earl of Oxford's widow. (Part of the collection was later purchased to form the basis of the British Library.) Henry Flitcroft was commissioned to create the gallery and saloon, and the drawing room is the work of Sir John Soane. Victorian additions by Kendall were later removed.

After a short time in the ownership of the Duke of Newcastle and his heir, the 2nd Earl of Oxford, in the early 18th century, the Hall was bought by the 1st Earl of Harwicke. The 5th Earl was the last member of that family to occupy Wimpole Hall and in 1938 it was bought by Captain George Bambridge and his wife Elsie, one of Rudyard Kipling's daughters. By this time it was almost derelict and most of the contents of the house had been sold.

It was the Bambridges who decided to demolish most of Kendall's Victorian additions, making the house more faithful to its original design. They then set about the mammoth task of restoring and furnishing the Hall, and it was their loving care and tireless hard work that made Wimpole what it is today. On Mrs Bambridge's death in 1976 the property was bequeathed to the National Trust.

One of the most stunning rooms is Sir John Soane's Yellow Drawing Room, but it is in very close competition with the magnificently decorated baroque chapel in the east wing, with its *trompe-l'oeil* ceiling, this time the creation of Sir James Thornhill. In contrast to all this finery, a glimpse of 'life below stairs' can be seen in the dry store, butler's pantry and the housekeeper's room in the basement.

If the Hall is remarkable for the number of great architects employed there, then the surrounding parkland can make a similar claim. It was transformed by no less than four of the country's most renowned landscape designers – Charles Bridgeman, 'Capability' Brown, Sanderson Miller and Humphrey Repton. The historic Home Farm, designed by Sir John Soane and including a range of buildings and rare breeds of farm animals, is also open to the public.

Open from mid-March to October on most days. Tel: 01223 207257.

*The River Great Ouse, in whose waters, it is said, lies the church spire*

# HEMINGFORD GREY
## *Cambridgeshire*

### 3 MILES (5 KM) EAST OF GODMANCHESTER

*Joseph came to a little sunlit place where there were yew bushes cut into the shapes of chess men. The castles had battlements round the top. With constant clipping the walls were solid...There was a door in the bastion...He felt a passionate longing to go in. (The garden of the manor house, described by Lucy Boston in The Castle of Yew (1965). The house and garden are open by appointment.)*

The banks of the River Great Ouse make a pretty setting for a lovely village, and in particular for a very special manor house. This is the oldest continuously inhabited house in England. In about 1130 its Norman owner built a two-storeyed house consisting of a storeroom on the ground floor and a hall above, entered by an outside staircase. The original Norman windows survive, as does a huge fireplace inside. The garden is bounded by the river on one side and a moat on the other three. The hall has been added to over the ages, but it remains a quite enchanted place and its last owner, Lucy Boston, used it as the setting of her classic *Green Knowe*

children's novels. Twelfth-century Norman stonework also survives in the solid round pillars in the north arcade of the village church. Other parts of the building date from the 13th century, including the beautiful double piscina with intersecting arches and mouldings. Outside, one cannot fail to notice the oddly truncated spire on top of the buttressed tower. Unlike Beeby's (see page 74), this spire was finished, but was blown down by a storm in 1741. The stump was then topped by decorative ball finials. There is a morass of undistinguished modern housing in the village, but at its heart are several striking houses of the 16th to 18th centuries.

# SWAFFHAM PRIOR
## *Cambridgeshire*

5 MILES (8 KM) WEST OF NEWMARKET

Twin churches sitting in tandem, diagonally placed in exact parallel across the square of one small churchyard: quite how this unusual phenomenon came about is a subject of speculation. Are they testimony to the rival endowments of two lords of the manor? Or, as some say, two embittered sisters? St Cyriac's dates from the 13th century but was rebuilt, except for the tower, early in the 19th century. It fell into decay but is now restored for use as a social centre, though for a time, when St Mary's spire was struck by lightning in 1767, this was in use and St Mary's was closed. St Mary's is more exciting, and particularly its tower. At its base it is very square Norman, next is an octagonal stage, also Norman, and then it goes 16-sided; all very powerful. Inside is an arresting series of early 20th-century stained-glass scenes depicting a World War I trench, an ammunition factory, Wicken Fen, and a Swiss mountain. The village street below the churchyard consists mainly of neat cottages and Georgian houses. Swaffham Prior House is mid-18th-century, of yellowish brick, while Baldwin Manor, on the outskirts, is a very lovely Tudor half-timbered house. The village also boasts two recently restored windmills, one of which turns again.

*St Mary's tower – a fibreglass spire replaces the original, which fell in the 18th century*

### The Devil's Dyke
Just to the north-east of the village the road comes to the Devil's Dyke, a colossal Romano-British or Anglo Saxon earthwork. The bank and the ditch are 40yds wide, from the top of the bank to the bottom of the ditch it is 60ft (18m), and the total length is 7 miles (11km). Walk along it (the Devil's Dyke Morris Men choose to dance the distance) and you will appreciate that that is a lot of earth to move with your pick-axe and shovel.

# CROSSING HOUSE
*Cambridgeshire*

SHEPRETH, 8 MILES (13 KM) SOUTH OF CAMBRIDGE

Although Crossing House has a small garden, there are more than 5000 species to be seen and the greenhouses are packed with unusual plants. It must also be one of the best known of country gardens, as it stands alongside the level crossing at Shepreth on the busy Cambridge-to-Royston railway line. The beauty of the garden, cultivated by Mr and Mrs Douglas Fuller over the past 30 years, and the half mile of railway embankment that they also care for, must have raised the spirits of many a traveller on this railway line.

As a conscious decision, the owners have decided to ensure that the visitor has something of interest to see whatever the time of year. Plant experts have identified 35 varieties of snowdrop at Crossing House, giant forms and those with green and yellow tips, while early spring produces drifts of naturalised crocuses, including *Crocus tommasinianus* 'Whitewell Purple', and many varieties of scillas. These are replaced as the season progresses by alliums, hardy terrestrial orchids like *Dactylorrhiza foliosa*, with its spikes of bright purple or pink flowers, Shirley poppies and flax.

Clematis provides summer colour, and there are many varieties of roses, some of them fragrant. Raised limestone beds hold alpines. During the autumn, Japanese anemones, colchicums and schizostylis, and the Kaffir lily are eye-catching, especially 'Viscountess Byng' with its pink flowers. Even in winter there is much to see, as rare hellebores, early crocus and irises are in flower during a mild period, as are viburnums and winter jasmine.

Although the soil at Shepreth is alkaline, rhododendrons, azaleas and pernettyas have been planted in containers of lime-free compost, and several varieties of Asiatic gentians are also grown in a trough. Two ponds have been added to the layout, and one has become a haven for wildlife, with frogs, toads and newts in residence. One of the three greenhouses is stocked with alpines, lewisias being strongly represented, while the others hold South African bulbs, many of them grown from seed, and also leptospermum, especially 'Burgundy Queen' with its dark-red flowers, and 'Keatleys', which is pink. It is surely remarkable what can be achieved in a small space in this country garden, from the dwarf box-edging to beds, to great yew arches, and the beauty of the scene must give encouragement to us all.

Open daily throughout the year. Tel: 01763 261071.

*Left, an inspiration to commuters, the Crossing House shows just what can be done with a small garden*

*Above, the garden extends along the trackside – though this part is out of bounds to visitors*

*Deutsche Budesbahn class 52 2-10-0 No 7173 receives a final check-over*

# NENE VALLEY RAILWAY
## *Cambridgeshire*

### WANSFORD, 8 MILES (13 KM) WEST OF PETERBOROUGH

The Nene Valley Railway has been a major asset to feature film makers, since it is the only railway in Britain which has such an extensive overseas collection – locomotives and rolling stock from 11 different countries can be seen here. Well-known films whose 'foreign' railway sequences were shot on the Nene Valley line include *Octopussy*, with Roger Moore as James Bond, *The Dirty Dozen* and *Murder on the Orient Express.*

This diverse collection was acquired partly by accident but also through necessity. By the time moves were afoot in the early 1970s to preserve a stretch of the railway along the Nene Valley, the only available locomotives in Britain were those languishing in Barry scrapyard in south Wales. Having been exposed to salt air for years, they were a costly proposition to restore. Moreover, Peterborough Development Corporation, which had bought the line from British Rail,

wanted to see trains running quickly. An offer of a Swedish engine seemed to be the answer to the problem, not least because it was necessary to demolish only one overbridge to make the line useable by locomotives built to the larger continental loading gauge. The Nene Valley soon attracted other foreign engines, and visitors can see examples from France, Germany, Austria, Poland, Sweden and Denmark. The railway also has a good collection of British engines, if the propensity to stick all the plumbing outside the boiler is not to your taste.

This line is very good for children. It has a locomotive permanently named *Thomas*, bestowed by the Reverend W Awdry himself, and young visitors particularly relish the tunnel. There is also the 2000-acre (800ha) Nene Park – an ideal place to break the journey, and served by the intermediate station at Ferry Meadows – which has play areas for children, a miniature railway, cycle

hire, nature trails and picnic sites.

Most passengers start their journey at the line's headquarters at Wansford, where you can also look round the engine shed. The original station building – an architectural gem in Jacobean style by the accomplished architect William Livock – is sadly not owned by the Nene Valley Railway, although their signal box is one of the finest on a preserved railway. Trains head west through the 671yd (614m) Wansford Tunnel to the site of Yarwell Junction, where the lines to Rugby and Northampton divided. Here trains reverse and head back through Wansford, cross the river and turn into the 3-mile (5km) straight to Ferry Meadows. Passing broad cornfields, followed by the man-made country park, the line terminates at Orton Mere in Peterborough, a short walk from the British Rail station.

Train service: Sundays from January to March, weekends from April to October, and a variable midweek service from June to August. Santa specials. Tel: 01780 782921.

*Crowds eagerly await the arrival of* Thomas

*Narrowly rescued from demolition, Oxburgh owes its continued existence to a persistent Lady Bedingfeld*

# OXBURGH HALL
## *Norfolk*

OXBOROUGH, 7 MILES (11.5 KM) SOUTH-WEST OF SWAFFHAM

*O*xburgh Hall has its roots firmly in the medieval era. Built for the Bedingfeld family in 1482, it has mellow stone walls rising sheer from the waters of its moat, and a great Tudor gatehouse. But Oxburgh's history is not only a long one, it has also experienced moments of danger and excitement. The fact that the house has survived at all is, indeed, little short of miraculous.

After the Civil War it was ransacked by Cromwell's men who set fire to part of it. Much later, in 1951, financial difficulties beset the family and after 500 years of the Bedingfeld family's occupation Oxburgh Hall was sold to a development company. Three months later that company put it up for auction, with the only prospective buyer being a demolition firm. However, at the eleventh hour, on the morning of the sale, Lady Bedingfeld raised enough money to make a successful bid and bought the house back.

There are portraits of the Bedingfeld family throughout the house, and the wonderful 17th-century wall-coverings of embossed and painted Spanish leather on the corridor and stairs are a notable feature. The King's Room, named in honour of a visit by Henry VII in 1497, now contains wall hangings embroidered by Mary, Queen of Scots and Elizabeth, Countess of Shrewsbury.

Open from late March to October on selected days. Tel: 01366 328258.

# CASTLE RISING CASTLE
## *Norfolk*

CASTLE RISING, 5½ MILES (9 KM) NORTH-EAST OF KING'S LYNN

In the castle grounds there are the remains of an 11th-century chapel. Their position, half covered by earthworks, suggest that the chapel was destroyed in order to make way for the castle.

*I*n 1327 the unfortunate King Edward II was horribly murdered in Berkeley Castle on the orders of his wife, Queen Isabella, and her lover, Roger Mortimer. At this time, Edward's heir, Edward III, was only 15 years old, and Mortimer and Isabella were able to rule England together by manipulating the young King. This state of affairs continued for three years until Edward III began to take matters back into his own hands. Learning of the roles of his mother and Mortimer in the death of his father, Edward had Mortimer tried for treason and hanged in 1330. Isabella, as guilty as Mortimer, was spared trial and execution, but was banished from the court. She spent the last 30 years or so of her life at Castle Rising, joining an order of nuns called the Poor Clares in her old age.

Although it is easy to look at the strong walls of the mighty keep at Castle Rising and imagine the fallen Queen confined, lonely and forgotten in her castle prison, there is no evidence that she was physically constrained there. In fact, there is some suggestion that she regularly toured around the area. It is more likely that Isabella's long sojourn at Castle Rising was her own choice, and that living out her days in the quiet peace of Norfolk was her penance for her part in the brutal murder of her husband.

There are many fascinating points about Castle Rising. As late as the 18th century, paintings of the castle show ships in the background, for when the castle was built in the 12th century it was near the sea, or at least accessible from the sea. No visitor to Castle Rising can fail to notice the massive Norman earthworks that surround the castle. Great ditches and mounds were thrown up, with walls added later, and still today – even without the threat of archers sending out hails of arrows – the grassy earthworks are difficult to scale.

The mighty, square keep was built between 1138 and 1140, although alterations to entrances and fireplaces were carried out later, and several rooms remain in excellent condition. They include a handsome wall passage and a chapel, complete with a small wall cupboard, on one of the upper floors. There is a well in the basement of the main tower and another in the castle grounds.

Open all year daily, except Christmas and New Year. Tel: 01553 631330.

*The castle is famous for its connection with Edward II's queen, Isabella*

# BURNHAM THORPE
## *Norfolk*

6 MILES (9.5 KM) WEST OF WELLS-NEXT-THE-SEA

This is the birthplace of Horatio Nelson. Burnham Thorpe is quietly proud of its son, England's greatest naval hero, but has never allowed itself to be degraded by any sort of souvenir industry. The pub and the church have plenty of Nelson memorabilia, but elsewhere the old flint village seems to carry on with life quite ordinarily. The Lord Nelson looks much as it must have done when he held a party here before setting off on HMS *Agamemnon* to fight Napoleon – except, that is, for the publican's admirable collection of Nelsonia. Next door is a handsome flint barn, probably a warehouse when the stream beside it was a tidal, navigable river. Locals say that Nelson's mother gave birth to him here, being unable to make it home to the rectory in time. The official story is that he was born, in 1758, in the old rectory, the site of which is marked with a plaque. A little north of the village centre is the church where Horatio's father was parson. The lectern and cross are made from timber from HMS *Victory*, and flags from the ship hang in the nave. The church itself dates from the 13th century. Do not miss the beautiful decorative flintwork on the exterior of the east wall.

*The flint walling of a cottage in the village, typical of this part of Norfolk*

**The Nelson Connection**
The village is only a few miles from the north Norfolk coast, off which Nelson may have learnt to sail as a young boy. He joined the navy in 1770, aged 12, and served in the Arctic, the East and West Indies and in North American waters during the War of Independence.
In 1788 he was back here again, with his wife Fanny, farming to supplement his half-pay for the five years until war broke out with France.

The Peddars Way is a Roman track that may well have been built on the route of an even more ancient, Celtic track. It is now a long-distance path that runs from Knettishall Heath, just over the Suffolk border, north-west to Holme next the Sea. Castle Acre is the only village of note as it makes its way across the Breckland and the remote north-west corner of Norfolk.

*The 11th-century Bailey Gate at Castle Acre*

# CASTLE ACRE
## *Norfolk*

### 4 MILES (6.5 KM) NORTH OF SWAFFHAM

Castle Acre is a good stopping-off place for walkers on the ancient Peddars Way. The Normans, however, did more than break their journey here. They built in a big way, and the ruins we are left with now are some of the most evocative in the land. William the Conqueror's son-in-law, William de Warenne, built a huge castle within the outer bailey of which much of today's village stands. Apart from the strikingly massive earthworks, little but its gateway remains. However, in 1090 Warenne built a Cluniac priory here and it is for this rather than the castle that Castle Acre is known. It was damaged badly in the dissolution, but one look at its soaring west front and the intricate decoration of its blind arcading and it takes only a little imagination to visualise what a thing of splendour this must have been. The Prior's Lodging is the only part of the building to have kept a roof. Many of the brick-and-flint houses of the village are built of material from the castle and priory ruins (both of which are in the care of English Heritage). Some buildings are new, many are 19th-century, one or two are medieval and the Ostrich Inn is 18th-century. Everything pulls together to make this a most attractive place.

# BURE VALLEY RAILWAY
## *Norfolk*

*With its headquarters at Aylsham, the BVR runs over the old Great Eastern Wroxham–Aylsham line*

WROXHAM, 7 MILES (11 KM) NORTH-EAST OF NORWICH

When the writer and broad-caster Miles Kington opened the Bure Valley Railway in 1990, it marked the completion of the longest miniature railway to be built in Britain since the 1920s. The 9-mile (14.5km) line links the 'capital' of the Norfolk Broads at Wroxham with the town of Aylsham, where the market square is ringed with fine 18th-century houses, and it serves a local transport function as well as being a tourist attraction. Conveniently, the British Rail and Bure Valley stations at Wroxham are connected by a foot-bridge, and the town centre at Aylsham is only a short walk from the station.

The 15in (375mm) gauge railway is built on the trackbed of a Great Eastern Railway branch line that left the Norwich to Cromer line at Aylsham and meandered through gently rolling country to join the Dereham–Wells line at the isolated junction of County School. Although the line was open for freight until the early 1980s, 17 bridges had to be repaired, a ¼-mile (0.5km) tunnel built under the Aylsham bypass and 6000 tons of crushed shingle brought in to replace the ballast.

The journey in the comfortable carriages takes visitors past the walls of the Elizabethan Little Hautbois Hall, its blocked-up windows still recalling the aesthetic damage done by the

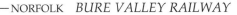

window tax, which was in force from 1695 to 1851. Heading for Aylsham, the train soon runs parallel to the River Bure, where swans can sometimes be seen in majestic flight and geese are ten a penny. The village of Buxton with Lammas, the two separated by the Bure, is served by a station on the line and an interesting place to break the journey. The attractive Church of St Andrew can be glimpsed from the train, but the Quaker Burial Ground and resting place of the author of *Black Beauty*, Anna Sewell, has to be sought out.

After rattling through the tunnel into Aylsham station, the train draws to a halt under a huge overall roof, a very grand terminus for a railway of this small gauge. The engine shed beside the station gives visitors the opportunity to admire the fine collection of surprisingly powerful locomotives, the most recent additions being based on an Indian Railways' narrow gauge design. Keen walkers can use their legs in either direction, since the line runs alongside the Bure Valley Walk; this path connects with a network of paths from Norwich and North Walsham created by Broadland District Council. Guides to the routes are available.

Train service: most days from Easter to end September. Santa specials. Tel: 01263 733858.

*Winson2-6-2 No 6, built in 1994, is the newest locomotive in service on the line*

# MANNINGTON HALL GARDENS
*Norfolk*

SAXTHORPE, 18 MILES (29 KM) NORTH-WEST OF NORWICH

Only 7 miles (11 km) from the sea in the open, rolling countryside of North Norfolk is the romantic Mannington Hall. Purchased in the 18th century by the brother of Sir Robert Walpole, the lovely medieval moated house is still owned by the Walpole family. Although the gardens are being extended, there are a number of areas to interest the garden lover, especially the Heritage Rose Garden – a deliciously scented layout – and a wild valley planted with unusual trees.

Walking across the spacious lawns towards the house, it is clear that the recent storms have badly damaged some of the great cedars, but fast-growing wellingtonias have been planted to replace those lost. Inside the Victorian 'battlement' walls, the borders are overflowing with herbaceous plants and roses, with *Rosa* 'Canary Bird' showing its

*The exuberant architecture of Mannington Hall makes a fine background for its celebrated collection of roses*

single yellow blooms in late spring. The bed beneath the house wall has peonies and lupins, while on the wall itself is a fine climbing hydrangea, *H. petiolaris*, and opposite is a splendid weeping pear with grey-green leaves.

Around the corner of the house *Rosa banksiae* 'Lutea' climbs vigorously close to a mauve wisteria, while rock roses brighten up the gravel with their pink and white flowers in early summer. A formal rose garden dominated by hybrid teas and with a sundial in the centre is surrounded by juniper. Within the moat an intricate pattern of sweetly scented herbs are planted underneath urns, filled with hyacinths in spring and replaced by brightly coloured pelargoniums later on.

Fruit trees line the intimate enclosure of the Heritage Rose Garden, which is divided into several areas, each representing a period of the rose's historical development. In all there are more than 1000 different varieties, including a wide range of wild roses. The Medieval Garden has turf seats and some very old roses, including *Rosa gallica* 'officianalis', and *R. spinosissima* stand near a small yew tree. Beyond the other formal areas of Mannington Hall, which include a tranquil 17th-century knot garden, is a spectacular wild valley. Here, in a totally different mood, there are many fascinating trees, including seven specimens of *Acer palmatum* which are well over 100 years old.

Open from Easter to October, on Sunday afternoons. Tel: 01263 584175.

# CLEY NEXT THE SEA
## *Norfolk*

### 4 MILES (6 KM) NORTH-WEST OF HOLT

The name is pronounced to rhyme with 'why' and it is not next to the sea any more, and has not been since the reclaiming of marshland for pasture in the 17th century left it a mile or so inland. In earlier days Cley was an important port at the mouth of the River Gleven, ranking second only to King's Lynn on this coast. Wool and later cloth was exported to the Netherlands, and the boats brought Dutch tiles back. There is still a small quay on the Gleven, but Cley's most notable feature today is the tremendous 18th-century wind-mill, with its sturdy brick tower, soaring white sails and conical wooden cap. One of the most photographed windmills in the country, it has been turned into a

**Blakeney Point**

A minor road runs northwards from Cley through the marshes to Cley Eye on the coast. From here there is a walk of three miles or so over the narrow shingle spit to the nature reserve at Blakeney Point, which belongs to the National Trust. It is a place of lonely and eerie beauty, a magnet to both botanists and birdwatchers, with its mudflats and saltmarshes , sandy hillocks and hollows, and spreading lawns of sea lavender. There's a colony of seals here in winter, terns innumerable nesting in summer with oystercatchers, redshank and other birds, and migrants coming through in spring and autumn. Blakeney Point can also be reached by boat from Blakeney Quay or Marston.

*Cottages, hollyhocks and a burgeoning garden at Cley*

*Kippers being smoked in obedient rows at Cley*

*The Whalebone House has inset panels of flints in whalebone frames*

private house and there has recently been some concern about its preservation. Among attractive houses of flint and red brick in the village is the unusual Whalebone House, with panels of flint in the walls framed by whalebones. To the south, where the old harbour stood, the church of St Margaret is one of Norfolk's finest, rebuilt on a grand scale in the 14th century and a witness to Cley's prosperity at that time. The Black Death in the l340s caused the money to run short, and so there is a much smaller chancel than the ample nave might lead you to expect. The two-storey 15th-century porch has fantastic battlements and a fan-vaulted roof, whose bosses are carved with angels and flowers and a woman throwing her distaff at a fox to scare it away from her chickens. The church has numerous fine brasses, including those of John Symonds and his wife in their burial shrouds, with the ominous words 'Now Thus', and their eight children. The transepts have been in ruins since Tudor days. Cley is on the part of the North Norfolk coast known to geologists as the North Alluvial Plain, a strip of land along the sea's edge, not more than 2 miles (3km) deep and built up over the last thousand years by sediment brought down by the rivers. Local landowners and farmers helped to create it by building walls and digging ditches to transform the salt-marshes into pastureland. The landscape mingles cattle pasture with saltmarshes through which creeks wind their way muddily to the sea among banks of shingle and sand. Birds haunt the area in multitudes, and almost the entire coastline is protected by nature reserves.

# CLEY MARSHES &
# BLAKENEY POINT

### Visitors to Cley
In addition to its human visitors, Cley plays host to large numbers of migrant birds during spring and autumn. Many of these are common species but birds like white-rumped sandpiper, slender-billed gull and rock sparrow are just some of the mouth-watering species that have turned up in the past few years. Cley is also Britain's most legendary site for vagrant birds, because of its position, protruding into the North Sea.

*This attractive walk is approximately 3 miles (4.8km), or up to 7 miles (11 km) for the longer route. The walking is generally level, but with some shingle to negoti-ate, especially on the Blakeney Point section. The walk begins at The Eye car park, north of Cley village, along a side-road towards the sea wall. Cley Marshes, a block of reed-beds, lagoons and pools is exceptionally good for wading birds and other marshland specialities. The coast is also renowned for its migrants in spring and, especially, in autumn. Blakeney Point is famous for rare migrants and good for sea views and salt-marsh.*

❧❧❧❧

### DIRECTIONS
**1 At the western side of The Eye car park, above the road-end, is a grassy bank with a path along the top.** This is the West Bank, separating the reclaimed marsh from the saltings. Turn left along the path and follow it towards Cley village.

The well-preserved windmill is Cley's most distinctive feature. The muddy creeks of the salt-marsh are hidden beneath a quilt of sea purslane. This stretches as far as the eye can see to the west, framed on one side by the wooded rise around Blakeney church and on the other by the long shingle ridge of Blakeney Point. The building just visible along the Point is called the Watch House, but is known to most birdwatchers as Half-way House.

**Continue along the West Bank.** The mournful cries of wading birds such as redshanks, greenshanks, curlews and grey plovers ring around the marshes all the time. Waders evolved these contact-calls to carry across open spaces, and the sounds resonate wonderfully.

The West Bank follows the road, with a narrow ribbon of reeds between the two. Opposite the small pool and sluice-gate it is a good idea to descend and follow the road, but if you have boots you can carry on a little further, until the bank angles westwards, then drop down to the road. The pool sometimes holds a few ducks, and the bushes beside it always seem to attract one or two autumn migrants such as barred and icterine warblers.

**2 Turn left (away from the village) where the beach road meets the main coast road.** Cars are not usually travelling fast, but take care and try to keep on the grass verge.

It is easy to be distracted by birds over the marshes to your left, but the views are poor at first because the road is barely higher than the reeds. A path above a car park on the right leads up to the Norfolk Naturalists Trust visitor centre, from where a permit may be bought to use the hides dotted around the marsh, which is well worth while. Some birds, such as passage warblers, crakes and rails, and the nesting avocets, are only seen properly by entering the reserve

**Continue along the roadside.** Off the road are several public hides which give better views over the marshes. Carter's

*Looking back across the creek towards Cley village*

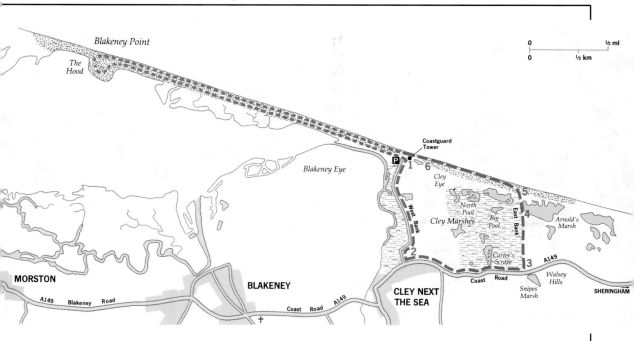

Scrape is one of the larger areas of mud and open water which is good for passage waders (ruffs, greenshanks etc.) and marsh terns if there are any about. After ¾ mile (1.2km) of road-walking you approach a scrub-covered hillside (Walsey Hills) with a reed-fringed pool (Snipes Marsh) on the right. For many years Walsey has been the site of a bird-ringing station and observatory, now run by the Norfolk Ornithological Association.

**3 There is a small car park on the left side of the road, just before Snipes Marsh, and next to it is another grassy bank leading towards the sea.** This is the East Bank – one of the best-known birdwatching spots in Britain. Walk along the path on the top of the bank.

To the right are grazing marshes, to the left is the Naturalists Trust reserve, of reed-beds and associated drains and channels. Many people walk straight along the East Bank, to reach either the reserve hides or the sea wall, but one of the most successful strategies can be to sit for a while in the grass and wait for birds to fly over. They always do; anything from bitterns to black terns, depending on the time of year. Even in mid-summer there are bearded tits, bitterns and harriers in the reed-beds. Drinker-moth caterpillars, cinnabar and burnet moths may share the grassy bank with you.

**4 Towards the end of the East Bank pass Arnold's Marsh, on the right.** This National Trust property used to be one of the best bird-watching places before the creation of all the other lagoons and scrapes, and it still attracts good numbers of wildfowl and waders.

**5 At the end of the East Bank turn left and walk either along the top of the sea wall or at its base.** The sea is sometimes worth watching for shearwaters, skuas etc, but it is less tiring to walk close to the marsh where the shingle is firmer underfoot.

**6 Continue along the sea wall, towards the coastguard tower, passing a stile to the Naturalists Trust hide and a small brackish pool with a wartime pillbox beside it.** This unattractive little pool has provided a haven for phalaropes and other storm-driven vagrants, and there are often one or two gulls, terns and plovers around it. **Return to The Eye car park.**

**7 The second, optional part of the walk now leads west along Blakeney Point.** To walk the 8 miles (13km) to the end of the Point and back needs considerable time and energy and is only recommended if you are fit and motivated. (A 1½–2 hour boat trip from Blakeney to Morston Quay is an enjoyable alternative in the summer, to see the tern colonies and the seals.) The Hood – about half-way along the Point – is as far as you really need to go.

The shingle ridge, colonised by yellow horned poppy, sea kale and spurrey, is the first landfall for birds on the move. When the winds have been in the east but the weather has deteriorated, thousands of migrants reach the beach in an exhausted state. Long-eared owls, woodcocks, wrynecks and a variety of other species can then be found here, drugged by tiredness and reluctant to fly. The scraps of cover sometimes carry hundreds of blackcaps, robins, goldcrests or redwings. In the winter there are usually a few snow buntings, shore larks or Lapland buntings about.

Return from The Hood along the landward side of the ridge; a path between the shingle and the mud offers an easier return route back to The Eye.

### A 'First' for Conservation

To the east of the village lies a great bed of reeds with brackish and freshwater lagoons. Designated Britain's first Local Nature Reserve in 1926, a further need for protection for the birds of Cley was realised – initially to stop the shooting of rare species for collections, and now from the hoards of birdwatchers who flock here each year.

### The Autumn Migration

August brings waders from the Arctic, September produces falls of wrynecks and other `European migrants heading south, as well as seabirds passing along the coast, and there is a special buzz of excitement in October as waifs and strays from Siberia make their first landfall.

Apart from the excitement of autumn, the best time to visit Cley is probably in late May or June, when avocets are nest-building, bitterns are booming, and terns and waders will be passing up and down the shore.

# NORTH NORFOLK RAILWAY

SHERINGHAM, 4 MILES (6.5 KM) WEST OF CROMER

*T*he 25-minute journey on the North Norfolk Railway might be an eye-opener for those who think of Norfolk as a flat county. For much of the outward journey over the 5¼ miles (8.5km) from Sheringham to Holt, the locomotive has to work hard on gradients as steep as 1 in 80, but the open embankments enable passengers to enjoy the marvellous views over the sea to the north and the woods inland.

*Lovely coastal views on the approach to Weybourne station*

Once part of the Midland & Great Northern Railway, the section that forms today's North Norfolk Railway was built to cater as much for holiday traffic as to serve local communities, but the seasonal nature of the line's income led to its downfall. It closed in stages between 1959 and 1964, although a new station at Sheringham can still be reached by train from Norwich and it is only a few minutes' walk between the stations. Re-opened to passengers in 1975, the original

Sheringham station reflects the number of passengers it handled when named trains like the *Broadsman* and *Norfolkman* called here. The elaborate cast-iron brackets supporting the canopy are adorned with hanging baskets, and there is plenty to look at while waiting for the next train, including a museum portraying the history of the Midland & Great Northern Railway.

After viewing the delightful landscape on the way to Weybourne, passengers will not be surprised to learn that it has been designated an Area of Outstanding Natural Beauty. Once a golf course on the seaward side is left behind, the land on either side is attractive arable country with fields of barley, carrots and sugarbeet. Inland the fields rise up to the

woodlands of Sheringham Park, landscaped by Humphry Repton, and regarded by him as his finest work. It is also interesting to see the railway from the park, from a viewpoint which puts the trains into the perspective of a fine panorama of coastline and agricultural hinterland.

The one intermediate station, at Weybourne, offers several reasons to postpone the final leg of the journey to Holt. It is here that locomotives are restored, and guided tours can be arranged by the stationmaster. A board on the station suggests walks through nearby Kelling Woods, and in the opposite direction, a mile from the station, is the village of Weybourne. As well as the ruins of an Augustinian priory and windmill, walkers are close to Weybourne Hope where exceptionally deep water made it a likely place for an attempted invasion in 1588 and again during World War II. The section to Holt climbs across Kelling Heath with good views out to sea. Although the station at Holt is yet to be developed, passengers in high season are often met by a horse-bus for conveyance into the Georgian market town.

Train service: daily from July to September; weekends in May; Sundays in March, April and October; also Easter week. Tel: 01263 822045.

Ring Haw *at Sheringham: the town also has a main line station with services to Norwich*

# THE BROADS

The Broads is the newest member of the National Park family, and
it has the youngest landscape. But if anyone had suggested just 40
years ago, when the first National Park was being designated, that
this enchanted area of mysterious, misty fens and slow, winding
waterways was anything other than natural, no-one would have
believed them. However, we now know that this entire network of
dykes and broads on the borders of Suffolk and Norfolk is entirely
man-made – and it is none the less beautiful for that. The area was
given long overdue protection when it was created a National
Park in all but name in 1989.

*The white-sailed Boardman's Windmill on the River Ant, near How Hill*

*Previous pages, a typical Broadland scene – the windpump, on the Berney Arms Reach which crosses Reedham Marshes*

The cormorants sat motionless on the windmill, silhouetted like two metal, cut-out weathervanes, one on the topmost edge of the sail and the other perched precariously on the tail vane. There was no danger that their belvedere would be disturbed, for the weather on that winter's day at How Hill, in the heart of the Broads, was misty, damp and eerily calm. The sinister black shapes of the cormorants seemed to remain in their commanding position for most of the seminar which I was attending at the How Hill environmental centre for the Broads, adding to the impression of their permanence.

The view from the Sun Room at How Hill was both a constant distraction and an inspiration during the long meetings, for, from its lofty heights – lofty, that is, for the low-lying Broads – the vista extended over the winding River Ant, the waving, tawny reedmarshes of Reedham, Clayrack and Bisley, and down to the red-brick towermill at Turf Fen. It was this glorious panorama which

Hill is still the highest point of the Broads National Park.

First recorded as 'Haugr', or 'Haugh Hill', meaning high point, it owes its name to the Viking invaders from Denmark who first nosed the inquisitive prows of their proud longships into the shallow staithe below the hill on the River Ant during the 9th century. The word *staithe* is found regularly along the east coast of England between Northumberland and Norfolk, and is pure Danish, meaning a quay, or landing point for ships. The view from How Hill was beautifully described by Walter White in a guidebook to Eastern England published in 1865:

> … a big knoll, thickly covered with oat-grass, from the top of which we had a pleasant view, and enjoyed the scent of elder blossom with which we had become familiar; broad reedy flats, pastures of various colour, coarse swamps, bright patches of poppies, irregular patches of water, windmills and dykes, and the narrow stream repeating its lazy curves across the vast level.

*The busy quayside at Wroxham, on the River Bure, is a major centre for boat hire on the Broads*

attracted Edward Boardman, the Norwich architect, and inspired him to build the charming Edwardian, reed-thatched and gabled house of How Hill as the family home.

How Hill itself is a prominent knoll of sand and gravel laid down in the outwash from a melting ice sheet during the Ice Ages. Once part of a much larger plateau, it was reduced to its present size by the abrasive action of the same glacial meltwaters which signalled the end of the Ice Age. At a mere 40ft (12m) above the sea, How

*Hickling, on Hickling Broad, is one of the quieter backwaters*

of the *Papilionidae* family, more usually found in the tropics, and makes a magnificent sight as it feeds on the flowers of campion and milk parsley.

During a break in the seminar we wandered down to How Hill staithe, inspecting the charming little former eel-catchers' cottage of Toad Hole on the way. This reed-thatched, red-brick two-up, two-down cottage, hidden away in the willows, has been faithfully reconstructed and furnished in traditional style by the National Park authority, and one half expects

He was describing a typical Broads landscape as it was before the invasion of tourism that began with the arrival of the railway in the 1870s.

But those marshy levels which ring How Hill remain some of the finest reedmarshes in Britain, and the home of rare, water-loving wildlife. Inhabitants include the mercurial hen harrier, which can often be seen quartering the reedbeds on floating, buoyant wings; the elusive bittern, whose booming notes echo across the marshes in the spring; the handsome bearded tit or reedling, and the more dowdy reed warbler, which builds its neat, circular nest using living reedstems as supports.

The huge wintering flocks of teal, wigeon, coot and redshank were the Norfolk wildfowlers' stock-in-trade in days gone by, and the spectacular swallowtail butterfly, Britain's biggest, still beats its showy way across the fen in high summer, attracting lepidopterists from all over the country. It is the only British member

to see Ratty and Mole appearing round the corner.

Moored up at the staithe was *Hathor*, a traditional Norfolk wherry sail boat. These broad-beamed, black-sailed wherries were the main form of cargo transport on the Broads for 200 years, but now the 23-ton *Hathor*, built at nearby Reedham in 1905, plies a charter trade for tourists along with a handful of other such craft. On board was skipper Peter Bower, passing the time of day with Eric Edwards, one of the last reed-cutters still employed on the Broads. The top-quality Norfolk reed is still in high demand for thatching all over the country, and Eric was looking forward to a busy harvest.

It took the combined research skills of a geographer, a botanist and a geomorphologist to finally crack the code which explained the creation of the Broads. Until then, less than 40 years ago, the enchanted, wet wilderness of the Broads had been regarded as an entirely natural landscape.

In fact, the 117 square miles (303 sq km) of the Norfolk Broads National Park, centred around three major

*Hickling Broad, with its wide expanse of reedbeds, is a National Nature Reserve and a haven for wildlife*

rivers, the Bure, the Yare and the Waveney, and their tributaries, the Ant, the Thurne and the Chet, which all meander down to the sea at Great Yarmouth, have been said to represent the greatest human modifications ever made to the natural landscape of this country. Geomorphologists had noted from borings that the original sides of the water-filled basins of the Broads were almost vertical and cut directly through the natural peat of the valley floors. Also, some Broads contained narrow, parallel peninsulas of peat, and islands whose sides were also steeply sloping or vertical. All this pointed to the fact that they were man-made; but where was the historical evidence? The answer to that question came from historians carefully sifting through the records of St Benet's Abbey, on the banks of the River Bure at Holme. The lonely, romantic ruins of this Benedictine monastery (a favourite subject for Victorian artists) are dominated by the 18th-century, round, red-brick towermill built inside the gatehouse. St Benet's, one of the most important historic sites in the Broads, probably dates from the 9th century, but was rebuilt and

*The 'Helter Skelter House' at Potter Heigham is the truncated remains of a Yarmouth fairground ride*

endowed with three manors by King Canute in AD1020.

The records showed that from the 12th century onwards certain areas in Hoveton parish were set aside for peat-digging, and in one year alone no fewer than a million turves were cut. This large-scale extraction, mainly for fuel, went on continuously for over two centuries, and by the early 14th century the cathedral priory at nearby Norwich alone was using nearly 400,000 turves annually from the area we now know as the Broads.

The total area excavated by those medieval peat-diggers has been estimated at about 2,600 acres (1,052ha), and the transformation of the 12ft (4m) deep peat-diggings to Broads resulted from gradual flooding from the 13th century onwards. At about this time there was a very slight change in the relative levels of the land and sea, and coastal and low-lying areas became increasingly at risk from flooding. Although there were some attempts to dredge peat under-water, using a special rake known as a

dydle, by the 15th century working had become so difficult that peat-cutting was no longer profitable and had been abandoned.

Since then, the shallow lakes have gradually been infilled with dead vegetation and sediment. Tithe maps of the 1840s show an area of nearly 3,000 acres (1,214ha) of open water, whereas today's figure is more like half that total.

Until recently, the waters of the Broads supported a wide variety of water plants which form the basis of

*Another individualist's home on the River Thurne at Potter Heigham*

the aquatic food chain and in turn support a great variety of insects, small animals and fish. But by the 1950s a significant change had begun to occur, and the waterways became increasingly choked by a luxuriant growth of underwater plants and algae.

The reason for this change was that there had been an enormous increase in the nutrient levels of the water, due to effluent from sewage treatment works and the run-off from the increased application of fertiliser on adjacent farmland. The result was that the formerly crystal-clear waters of the

Broads were turned into a murky pea-soup by the floating algae – a process known to scientists as eutrophication.

The Broads authority has taken steps to halt this process by pumping out the enriched mud from the bottom of some Broads by suction dredging. The results, in places like Cockshoot Dyke and Cockshoot Broad, have been very encouraging, with a dramatic improvement in water quality and the re-establishment of submerged water plants such as waterlily, hornwort and bladderwort.

The 125 miles (200km) of lock-free navigable rivers and Broads in the

*A boathouse at Hickling, thatched with locally-grown Norfolk reed*

National Park make it one of the most intensively used inland waterways in Europe, and it has been estimated that there were more than 2,000 hire cruisers on the Broads in the mid-1970s. Some 200,000 holidaymakers now use weekly-let motor cruisers annually, and this is also a cause for concern to the Broads authority as the wash from motorised pleasure craft can break up the reed mats on the banks of the Broads, and eventually the banks themselves can be washed away. Artificial bank protection, the imposition of speed limits on boating, the isolation of certain stretches of

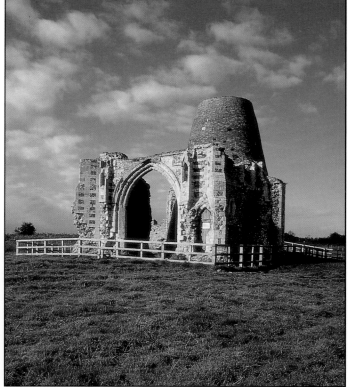

bank, and research into hull design are among the solutions currently being investigated.

In total, the Broads National Park receives over three million annual visitors, most of whom come to enjoy the unspoiled beauty of Broads, dykes and fens, the wet, tangled alder carr woodlands, and the wide expanses of grazing marshes under those vast East Anglian skies. Halvergate Marshes, just to the west of Great Yarmouth and bordering Breydon Water, could be said to be the birthplace of the Broads National Park, for in 1985 it became the site of the experiment which was to result in the first Environmentally Sensitive Area (ESA) in England. Here, farmers are paid to manage the extensive, windmill-dotted marshes by traditional grazing methods, and this should conserve their unique features for posterity.

When the idea of National Parks in Britain was being discussed in the 1940s, the eminent biologist Julian Huxley wrote from Paris saying that he could not imagine a group of British National Parks being set up which did not include the Broads. It took 40 years to happen, but now the Broads – that 'last enchanted land' – is an integral, important and very special member of Britain's National Park family.

*The ruins of St Benet's Abbey, on the River Bure near Ludham, where the secret of the Broads' creation was revealed*

*Defeated by the sea: the remains of the church at Eccles*

# ECCLES
## *Norfolk*

2 MILES (3 KM) NORTH OF LESSINGHAM

The village's name probably comes from the Latin word for a church, *ecclesia*, and it is thought that a church may have been constructed here originally far back in Roman times, soon after Constantine the Great's edict of toleration in AD313. This stretch of the Norfolk coast with its flat, sandy shore is particularly at risk from the sea, which invaded it regularly all through the 17th and 18th centuries. Defences were built of faggots, stones and clay, but it was not enough to save Eccles. The ruthless sea finally claimed the old village and its church of St Mary a hundred years ago. By 1858 the high tides swirled almost up to the tower of the church, which was partly buried in sand. In January 1895 a great storm finally destroyed the church completely, and all that is left now are tumbled boulders of flint masonry, lying on the beach as melancholy fragments of a lost past. The sand dunes above the beach have been planted with marram grass, to knot the dunes into a natural sea wall as protection against further encroachment by the waves. Behind this uncertain barrier are the few bungalows and beach chalets of present-day Eccles on Sea.

# CROMER
## *Norfolk*

21 MILES (34 KM) NORTH OF NORWICH

*I*n 1779 a bathing machine was advertised at Cromer, and soon the rich Norwich banking families of Gurney and Barclay and their Quaker relations began to take holidays here, and to rent or buy houses. The resort developed further in the 19th century. The sandy beach was an attraction, and so (it was said) were 'the simple manners of the inhabitants', the fact that the sun could be seen both rising and setting in the sea, and the local dressed crab. It was a place for gentlefolk, and there was opposition when the railway arrived in 1877. Hotels and lodging houses now proliferated, the journalist Clement Scott publicised this stretch of coast as 'Poppyland', and a new pier and bandstand were built in the 1900s. The earlier Cromer was a fishing village which took the place of an earlier one still, called Shibden, that was consumed by the sea. The impressive church of St Peter and St Paul, whose l60ft (49m) tower is much Norfolk's tallest, was built in the 14th century. Nearby cottages have been turned into a museum of the area's history and natural history. There is a lifeboat museum, too, and a richly old-fashioned seaside follies show still packs them in at the pier theatre through the summertime.

`You should have gone to Cromer, my dear, if you went anywhere. Perry was a week at Cromer once, and he holds it to be the best of all the sea-bathing places. A fine open sea, he says, and very pure air.'
Jane Austen, *Emma* (1815)

*The county's highest church tower soars up behind Cromer's seafront*

# HOLKHAM HALL
## *Norfolk*

2 MILES (3 KM) WEST OF WELLS-NEXT-THE-SEA

Thomas William Coke was a fervent supporter of the Americans during the War of Independence, and each evening he is said to have toasted George Washington as the 'greatest man on this earth'.

*'An Englishman's home is his castle.'*
First said by Sir Edward Coke

*Holkham is one of the greatest 18th-century houses in England*

The Coke (pronounced 'Cook') family were established at Holkham long before the present Palladian mansion was built. Their ancestor, Sir Edward Coke, was Attorney General to Elizabeth I and Chief Justice to James I, and his home was an Elizabethan manor house. When his descendant, Thomas Coke, returned from a six-year Grand Tour he realised that the manor was too small to accommodate the immense collections of works of art that he had accumulated. He had the house demolished and in 1743 a fine new classical-style Holkham Hall began to take shape which would suit his acquisitions.

The Marble Hall is modelled on a Roman Temple of Justice, and in the north dining room, tablets on the chimneypieces depict two of Aesop's Fables, *The Bear and the Beehive* and *The Sow with her Litter and the Wolf*. The state gallery has a superb collection of classical sculpture, including a statue of Diana and a bust of Thucydides which date back to about 4BC.

Perhaps the most famous member of the family is Thomas William Coke, better known as 'Coke of Norfolk'. A patron of agricultural inventions, and Member of Parliament for Norfolk, he was also responsible for the planting of no less than a million trees at Holkham.

Open from June to September daily, except Friday and Saturday. Tel: 01328 710227.

# KING'S LYNN
## *Norfolk*

### 39 MILES (63 KM) WEST OF NORWICH

The civic treasures of Lynn can be admired in the 15th-century, chequered flintwork Trinity Guildhall: royal charters from 1204, regalia, maces, the superb King John loving cup. Known as Bishop's Lynn until Henry VIII confiscated it from the Bishop of Norwich, this old port on the Great Ouse, 3 miles (5km) inland from the Wash, is a place of character and charm despite the attentions of post-war planners. It grew around not one, but two market places, each close to the river and each with a noble medieval church. St Margaret's in the Saturday Market is famous for its elaborate 14th-century brasses, Baroque pulpit and 18th-century organ case. To the north is the Tuesday Market with St Nicholas's Church and St George's Guildhall (National Trust), another 15th-century edifice in chequered flint, now used as a theatre and the headquarters of Lynn's annual festival. Between the two, on the quay, is the graceful old Custom House. The Queen Street Museum displays Lynn's history and daily life from the 12th century to the 20th. Lynn Museum itself deals with regional history and wildlife, and there is a museum of the local fishing industry at True's Yard.

# GREAT YARMOUTH
## *Norfolk*

### 18 MILES (29 KM) EAST OF NORWICH

Like the Alde to the south, the River Yare heads for the sea – through the spreading sandflats and mudflats of Breydon Water – only to be deflected to the south by a narrow spit of land. It was on this peninsula that the port of Yarmouth developed, along the river and with its back turned firmly to the sea. Here the herring drifters landed their catches and the curing houses smoked the celebrated Yarmouth bloaters. Yarmouth was an active shipbuilding centre, but for centuries its prosperity rested mainly on the vast shoals of herring in the North Sea. Merchants from all over Western Europe and Scandinavia came to the medieval Free Herring Fair, which lasted for 40 days from Michaelmas. Before World War I more than a thousand fishing boats plied from Yarmouth, but overfishing eventually took its toll and the port turned to servicing North Sea oil and gas operations. There are also regular ferries to Holland, for Yarmouth is 20 miles (32km) nearer to Rotterdam than it is to London. Running inland from the quayside were the old, cramped alleys called the Rows, so narrow that a special horse-drawn vehicle called a troll cart, 12 feet (4m) long and only 3 feet (1m) wide, was developed for

moving goods in the town. In 1804 they were numbered, from Row 1 to Row 145. Yarmouth was badly damaged by bombing during World War II, but parts of the Rows survived, and the Old Merchant's House and Row 111 Houses (English Heritage) are open to the public. Sections of the medieval town walls also survive, and along the river quays are examples of merchants' houses from Tudor to Victorian times, including the grand 18th-century mansion of John Andrews, the herring king, which later became the Customs House. The 13th-century Tollhouse, with its dungeons, is a museum of local history, and the Elizabethan House is now a museum of 19th-century home life. Yarmouth today is Norfolk's largest town and East Anglia's most popular seaside resort. It turned round to face the sea in the 19th century, to exploit its miles of sandy beach. The two piers date from the 1850s, and the 'Northern Margate' is fully equipped with amusement arcades, funfair rides, bowling greens, seafront gardens and lively entertainment. The Maritime Museum for East Anglia, in a former home for shipwrecked seamen, deals with the area's maritime past, and a statue of Britannia crowns the 144ft (44m) Nelson's Monument.

### At Home in a Boat

Charles Dickens visited Yarmouth in 1848, and the town appears in scenes in *David Copperfield* (which came out in the following year), among them the dramatic shipwreck in which the villain, Steerforth, loses his life. Earlier in the story, Peggotty, the young David's nursemaid, takes him to her Yarmouth home in a superannuated boat with a door and windows cut in the sides and an iron funnel sticking out for a chimney. This delightful home has a strong fishy smell from the the lobsters and crabs in the outhouse, 'in a state of wonderful conglomeration with one another'.

*Two faces of Yarmouth – left, the sturdy south gate of the old town wall, and below, colourful holiday activity on the sands beside the Britannia Pier*

# ALDEBURGH
*Suffolk*

### 6 MILES (10 KM) SOUTH-EAST OF SAXMUNDHAM

*A fisherman and his boat on the shingle at Aldeburgh, where the sea ate much of the town*

The River Alde rises near Famlingham and makes its reluctant way eastwards until suddenly, within a hundred yards of the coast, it turns right and under the disapproving eye of a Martello tower wanders on to the south for another ten miles, parallel to the shore. Aldeburgh is immediately to the north of the river's right-hand bend. A minor seaside resort and fishing village, it is also a major musical centre, known since 1948 for the Aldeburgh Festival. The little half-timbered, flint-and-brick Moot Hall was built in Tudor times as the market hall, presumably in the middle of the market place. Now it stands almost on the shingle beach where the fishermen draw up their boats, and half the Tudor town has vanished into the maw of the sea. The building was heavily restored in 1854, when the Jacobean-style chimneys were added. Today's town extends along the coast down to Slaughden Quay on the Alde, where yachts and small boats tie up. There was ship-building here in the 16th and 17th centuries, and much smuggling in the 18th, when it was said that the parson was the only man in Aldeburgh who was not a smuggler. As well as smugglers, this part of the Suffolk coast also attracted writers, including

**Music Hath Charms**
The annual Aldeburgh Festival of Music and the Arts, originally presided over by Benjamin Britten and Peter Pears, has become a prestigious occasion since its foundation in 1948. Many of Britten's operas and other works were given their first performances at the festival. Some events are held in the church, but the main concert hall is in the Maltings at Snape, a few miles inland. Britten lived in a converted windmill at Snape and wrote *Peter Grimes* there before moving to Aldeburgh in 1947.

Wilkie Collins and Edward Fitzgerald, the author of the fatalistic *Rubáiyát of Omar Khayyám* – though he was far from fatalistic when a wave invaded his bathing machine. Carlyle wrote approvingly of Aldeburgh's shingly beach and clear water, and E M Forster enjoyed the bleakness of the place. It was a broadcast talk about Aldeburgh by Forster that drew Benjamin Britten back to the area. The doyen of Aldeburgh authors, however, is George Crabbe, the poet-clergyman whose grandfather was customs collector here and who was born in the town in 1754. It was from him that Britten took the story of Peter Grimes.

There is a bust of Crabbe in the flint church of St Peter and St Paul. Strolling actors used to put on plays in the church, including quite possibly William Shakespeare himself in 1595. Crabbe preached as a curate from the elaborately carved pulpit. Benjamin Britten, who died in 1976, is buried in the churchyard here, and the stained-glass window in his memory was designed by John Piper. Elizabeth Garrett Anderson, Britain's first woman doctor and a leading campaigner for women's rights, died in 1917 and is also buried here. She grew up in Aldeburgh and succeeded her father as mayor of the town.

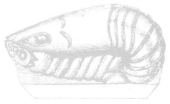

*The central rotunda of
Ickworth is unmistakable*

# ICKWORTH
*Suffolk*

2½ MILES (4 KM) SOUTH OF BURY ST EDMUNDS

*E*ven amidst all the excesses of the 18th century the design of Ickworth was unusual, with its great oval rotunda at the centre and two large wings curving out on each side. The brainchild of Frederick Hervey, the 4th Earl of Bristol and Bishop of Derry, it was designed to house his collections of art and other items, but sadly he did not live to see his creation completed; the finishing touches were not made until 27 years after his death. It is quite obvious, even from first sight of the building today, that it was intended first and foremost as a gallery, with any domestic requirements taking second place.

The Earl Bishop's descendants may often have felt that they had been left with something of a white elephant, but they completed the house and made what alterations they could to create a more practical place to live. Ickworth's virtue as a showcase for the family's superb art collections, however, has always been undisputed.

The house is filled with treasures: paintings by Velasquez, Lawrence, Kauffmann, Gainsborough and others; fine furniture and porcelain and one of the most splendid collections of silver in the country. Some of the décor itself is an art form, as in the wonderful Pompeian Room.

Open from Easter to October on selected afternoons. Tel: 01284 735270.

*The beautiful, moated Otley Hall*

# OTLEY HALL
## *Suffolk*

### 7 MILES (11.5 KM) NORTH OF IPSWICH

*I*t would seem that this exquisite moated hall, which dates from the 15th century, has not always received the loving care and attention that must surely be its due. Built by the Gosnold family, who occupied it for some 250 years, it was then sold to the Rebows who let it on a lease for the next 200 years. Although this action prevented the kind of 'modernising' that freehold owners are likely to have carried out, the building was sadly neglected.

Just before World War I, however, a saviour came along in the shape of Mrs Arthur Sherston, who carried out much restoration work, remodelled the east wing and modernised the kitchen and the main block. After her death the Hall was unoccupied again for a time while difficulties with the inheritance were sorted out, and it soon fell into another period of decline.

Since 1950 successive owners have done much to restore the house and gardens and the present owner, John Mosesson, is continuing this worthwhile task. Richly carved beams, herringbone brickwork and decorative plasterwork are in abundance throughout the house, the oldest part of which is the south wing. There is some lovely linenfold panelling in the parlour, with mullioned windows in the Great Hall and splendid wall paintings in the banquet hall.

Open on selected days in spring and summer. Tel: 01473 890264.

# HELMINGHAM HALL
## *Suffolk*

STOWMARKET, 9 MILES (14.5 KM) NORTH-EAST OF IPSWICH

*A mauvy-blue delphinium from the herbaceous border*

Helmingham Hall is the home of the ancient Tollemache family. Standing serenely inside its deep moat, the mellow brickwork of the Tudor house is appropriately surrounded by a magnificent garden centred on à 19th-century parterre. This is edged with a beautiful spring border which leads into a lushly planted enclosure on the site of the old kitchen garden. Beyond this again is an orchard and apple walk; on the other side of the house is a historical knot and herb garden designed in 1982 for the Tollemaches by Lady Salisbury.

Entering the main gardens along a grassy causeway which runs between the house moat and the one which surrounds the parterre, you come at once to a rose garden filled with hybrid musks. Here, the familiar 'Penelope', 'Felicia', 'Pink Prosperity' and 'Buff Beauty' bloom alongside rarer varieties such as 'Danae', 'Daybreak' and 'Nur Mahal', and there are also American ones such as 'Bishop Darlington'. This part of the garden is

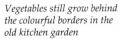

*Vegetables still grow behind the colourful borders in the old kitchen garden*

a wide rectangle with classical stone figures at each end, the banks dotted with primroses and narcissi in spring. The roses themselves grow in wide beds edged with Hidcote lavender and underplanted with London pride, which provides a carpet through which peonies, *Campanula latiflora* and alstroemeria also grow.

Through the gates of the walled garden, a central grassy path divides the area into eight beds, as it did when this was an Elizabethan kitchen garden. Bordered by herbaceous plants and backed by climbing roses, among them 'Albertine' and 'New Dawn', the vegetable plots are divided by walks and arched tunnels on which sweetpeas, gourds and runner beans grow. The main herbaceous borders are immensely colourful with acanthus, alliums, delphiniums, achillea and *Papaver orientalis*, while the Orchard Garden in spring is covered with primroses, cowslips, wild orchids and ox-eye daisies. The low box hedges of the knot to the east of the house contain herbs. There is also a magnificent collection of shrub roses mixed with campanulas, geraniums, foxgloves and lady's mantle. Enclosed by yew hedges, this is a beautiful garden where all the plants have been chosen to be contemporary with the house.

Open from May to September, on most Sunday afternoons. Tel: 01473 890363.

*Winged horse-heads stand proudly on the gate pillars of the walled garden*

Pargeting, the art of raised (or occasionally incised) decorative plasterwork, is quite commonly seen on façades and gables of timber-framed houses in the towns and larger villages of Suffolk, Essex and Hertfordshire. The technique, developed in the 16th and 17th centuries, was to *pour jeter* (throw) plaster over the timber-framing. Patterns were then applied by pressing moulds into it while it was still wet. Earlier examples usually depict plants, animals or people, while later designs tend to be more geometric.

# CLARE
## *Suffolk*

### 7 MILES (11 KM) WEST OF SUDBURY

*The Ancient House, a former priest's house next to the church, is dated 1473 – its pargeting would have been added much later*

*I*n the streets at the centre of this substantial village are many beautiful old houses, cottages and shops, some dating back to the 15th century. A number are exquisite examples of the local art of pargeting, their frontages bringing to mind delicately embroidered linen or an intricately iced cake. Like so many villages in this part of the country, Clare is a legacy of the enormous prosperity that came from the woollen cloth trade in the Middle Ages. Its origins, however, are in its Iron Age hillfort, near the church. Later, the Norman de Clare family, recognising its commanding position over the Stour valley, built a motte and bailey here which was to become the centre of the powerful empire known as the Honour of Clare. In 1248 Gilbert de Clare built an Augustinian priory on the banks of the river, the first of that order in England. It was dissolved in 1538, but in 1954 the monks returned and Clare is an Augustinian priory once more. The big flint church above the market place of this substantial village dates in part from the 13th century. Its medieval stained glass was mostly smashed in 1643 by the Puritan William Dowsing who went about East Anglia destroying 'pictures superstitious'. He left the heraldic pieces; he had no problems, presumably, with heraldry.

*A colour-washed corner of a village so unique that it is best explored out of season*

# KERSEY
## *Suffolk*

### 10 MILES (16 KM) WEST OF IPSWICH

K ersey, all of it, is just one street that runs down from its church on top of one hill, to a watersplash through a little river, and then steeply up again the other side to the ruins of a priory that crowned the hill opposite. From either end there is one of the most enchanting views to be found in Suffolk, across the red-tiled gables and rooftops of the ancient half-timbered houses. Many of the houses are pastel colour-washed, all leaning out and in and up against one another. The watersplash provided the running water needed for washing the Kersey cloth produced here in the late Middle Ages and every house was either the home of a cloth merchant or a weaver's cottage, in which there would have been a loom at work – this was literally a cottage industry. The church was built largely in the 14th century on this wealth, big and beautifully decorated within and without. Outside, there is ornate flint flushwork; the inside got beaten up a bit in the Reformation but some lovely things survive. By the stream is a 500-year-old house with a huge timber-framed doorway; in The Green are chocolate-box, pastel cottages; while opposite The White Horse is a group of timber-framed houses, with worn steps leading up to old oak doors and ancient bay windows.

The Swan Inn used to be a favourite of the American airmen of the 487th Bomb Group who were based in the area during World War II. It has a collection of wartime memorabilia and in one bar preserves a section of wall that is covered with the airmen's signatures.

Timber-frame construction in East Anglia is different from that of other areas in that many more vertical timbers are used than horizontal. The verticals are therefore placed quite close together, producing a totally different effect from the square chequerboard frontages seen in Cheshire or the Midlands. Notable by their absence in East Anglia are cruck and jointed-cruck trusses, used in every area of the country except the eastern counties.

*Little Hall, home of the Suffolk Preservation Society and the Gayer-Anderson Collection of paintings, ceramics and furniture*

# LAVENHAM
## *Suffolk*

### 6 MILES (9.5 KM) NORTH-EAST OF SUDBURY

This is the most famous, the most glorious, of all Suffolk's famous and glorious wool villages. In 1326 Edward III banned the import of foreign cloth, giving a boost to home industry and encouraging the immigration into East Anglia of Flemish weavers with whom there were already trading connections.

Through the 14th and 15th centuries Lavenham developed and prospered, rebuilding itself in appropriately wealthy style. After about 1600, however, little new building took place as Lavenham, along with other wool towns, began to decline. With the development of water-power for the fulling process, the weaving industry began to shift towards the hill streams of the west and north of England, and with the invention of the power loom dependent on water and then coal, weaving in East Anglia was finished. Lavenham reverted to agriculture and never became industrialised. The magnificent timbered cloth-halls, the fine cloth-merchants' houses, the beautiful guildhall, the quite splendid church, even the weavers' cottages have more or less all remained intact. Somehow, it is as though time has stood still for those medieval weavers and dyers and fullers.

To walk about Lavenham is to breathe its medieval perfection through every pore. Sailing above the village and the undulating countryside that nourished it is the great knapped flint church tower. This is a most spectacular church, built on the combined funds of a rich clothier, Thomas Spring, and the de Veres, Earls of Oxford. The interior is elaborate; of its finer detailing note, if nothing else, the charming carvings on the misericords (the pelican, especially) and the amazingly elaborate Spring family pew. They and their fellow cloth-merchants would have operated from the early 16th-century guildhall. Look closely at the exceptional quality of the decoration of its timbering and it is clear that Lavenham was no run-of-the-mill place. Notice particularly the carved corner posts of the porch. Also in the market place is Little Hall, another beautiful half-timbered building of the 14th century, the 500-year-old Angel Hotel and some Georgian remodelled frontages. The market cross has stood since 1501. The Swan Hotel now incorporates the old wool hall, another superb timbered building. But there are superb timbered buildings in every street, round every corner. Gables lean in or out, jetties slope up or down, roofs dip and rise. Suddenly a little carved head peeks out from under an eave. It has watched countless generations go by. It has always been there, one feels, and it surely always will be.

*The 16th-century guildhall*

*Old fishermen's cottages in Quay Street, which in Tudor times was under the sea*

# ORFORD
## *Suffolk*

### 9 MILES (14.5 KM) EAST OF WOODBRIDGE

**Musical Premières**

Several of Benjamin Britten's works had their first performances in the broad, lofty nave of Orford Church, notably *Noye's Fludde* (1958), based on the Chester miracle play and intended by the composer for performance in church with the audience participating in traditional hymns; and three one-act Church Parables, *Curlew River* (1964), *The Burning Fiery Furnace* (1968) and *The Prodigal Son* (1968).

Glance at a map or, better, look east from the top of the castle keep. Between Orford and the sea lie first the River Ore and then the 10-mile-long (16km) shingle bank of Orford Ness. This began to build up in the 16th century, gradually silting up the river and rendering the harbour useless for trade. Hence Orford's decline from a busy medieval port trading in wool with access to the open sea – and three churches, two hospitals and a friary – to today's pleasant and peaceful village of brick and timber-framing with a riverside quay popular with pleasure craft. Its castle keep, however, has stood oblivious to the vagaries of the Suffolk coast, since

Henry II had it built in 1165–7. There are two significant things about the castle (English Heritage). It was the first to be built with a keep that was cylindrical internally and 18-sided externally, the polygonal shape making it stronger and more easily defended than a square or rectangular one. Secondly, the financial records of the King's Exchequer, the Pipe Rolls, exist, meaning that this is the oldest castle for which there is documentary evidence. The ruined chancel of the village church is of similar date, the nave and tower being 14th-century. Especially attractive are the old market square and the street that leads down to the quay.

# WOODBRIDGE
## *Suffolk*

### 8 MILES (13 KM) EAST OF IPSWICH

*O*ne of Suffolk's most engaging small towns climbs a steep hill above the River Deben and the quayside, bustling with boatyards and small craft as it has time out of mind. The scene is dominated by the gleaming white Tide Mill. There has been a mill here since the 12th century. This one dates from 1793, worked until 1957 and is now a museum. It is operated by tidal water, artfully trapped in a pool behind the mill and used to drive the wheel when the tide has fallen. Visitors can see it working when the tide is right. At the heart of the town, the parish church of St Mary, with its noble 108ft (33m) tower of flint and stone, and a celebrated peal of bells, stands in a churchyard of tall trees and table tombs. Close by is the 16th-century Shire Hall, in red brick with a charming, curly Dutch gable. Notable inns include the King's Head and the 16th-century Olde Bell and Steelyard, with the steelyard itself sticking out above the street. It was used for weighing wagons and could lift a load of up to 2.5 tons.

*The serenely weather-boarded Tide Mill by the harbour at Woodbridge*

# NETHERFIELD HERBS
## *Suffolk*

ROUGHAM, 4½ MILES (6.5 KM) EAST OF BURY ST EDMUNDS

*Grassy paths lead between the neat box-edged beds*

Set deep in the Suffolk countryside near Bury St Edmunds is a small but very distinguished herb garden, Netherfield Herbs. The owner, Lesley Bremness, has been growing herbs and writing about them now for more than 20 years, and a visit to Netherfield undoubtedly deepens one's knowledge about the many uses to which herbs can be put – in cooking, in medicinal remedies and in cosmetics.

As soon as you enter there is a small enclosure which contains two cartwheels, one planted with many varieties of thyme, and the other spilling over with mint, the spokes making a natural division. Around the edges of the courtyard are more herbs, all carefully labelled, revealing, for instance, that lovage as an antiseptic can be applied to wounds, the roots of the musk mallow can cure coughs and urinary complaints, while parsley is rich in vitamins A, B and C. Beyond the 16th-century thatched cottage are two attractive box-edged knot gardens, the subtle foliage colours being provided by the silver curry plant, *Helichrysum augustifolium*, pale green santolina and the shiny evergreen leaves of teucrium.

Four demonstration beds in the centre of the densely planted herb garden are devoted to sages, rosemaries, oreganos, marjorams and

*A great variety of herbs, for culinary and medicinal use, are grown here*

thymes. The prostrate sage keeps its leaves late into the year, but the pineapple sage needs to be overwintered indoors. *Akebia quinata*, a hardy semi-evergreen, covers an arbour seat, and as well as being deliciously fragrant the tiny, purple-red flowers of this elegant climber turn into edible fruits if the summer has been a hot one. Near by is a pale pink, highly scented damask rose, the petals of which are used for rose oil and rosewater, while the tiny sweet briar, full of apple fragrance, stands over apricot-coloured foxgloves.

In one corner a golden hop is trained on to a cherry, underplanted with elecampane, the aromatic root of which Helen of Troy was supposed to have been collecting when she was abducted by Paris. Two 16th-century beds contain salad herbs – purslane and salad rocket – and medicinal herbs including blue and pink comfrey. A small statue of Pan beneath a weeping pear is surrounded by white and crimson roses, and there are also many culinary herbs to be found, including sweet cicely, tansy, broad-leaved sorrel and bible herb. This most enchanting garden does much to correct the general ignorance about these useful plants as well as giving pleasure to all with its scent and beauty.

Open daily.

# SOUTHWOLD
*Suffolk*

## 8 MILES (13 KM) EAST OF HALESWORTH

The lighthouse and the church tower both rise 100 feet (30m) into the sky over Southwold, on its cliff above the North Sea. The gleaming white lighthouse, standing among the houses of the town, dates from the 1880s. The church is some four hundred years older, with splendid examples of Suffolk 'flushwork' – patterns made of flint and stone. It was built here to replace a previous church which had burned down, and is dedicated to St Edmund, King and Martyr, because Southwold belonged to the rich abbey of Bury St Edmunds. St Edmund was a 9th-century East Anglian king, shot to death by the Danes with arrows, like a latter-day St Sebastian, when he refused to renounce his Christian faith. The church has a fine hammerbeam roof, and the painted figures in the panels of the rood and aisle screens have been restored. The choir stalls are among the finest in the county. The ancient figure of a man-at-arms, called Southwold Jack, with bloodshot eyes and a stubbly beard, is armed with a sword and a battleaxe with which he strikes a bell to herald services or salute a bride as she arrives on her wedding day. The *Domesday Book* records a substantial tribute of herrings sent to the monks of Bury St Edmunds every year from Southwold, and Buss Creek to the north of the

*Adnams' Brewery in Southwold delivers its ales in the old-fashioned way*

*A chorus-line of brightly painted bathing huts offers shelter from the east wind*

town is named after the 'busses', or herring boats. By the end of the 16th century the town's prosperity was in danger from the same sea from which it earned its living, as the tides threatened to block the harbour mouth with shingle and a cut had to be made through it. In 1659 the town caught fire and most of it was destroyed. It was rebuilt in a style which has a distinctly Dutch flavour. The Southwold Museum on Bartholomew Green has Dutch gables and an enjoyable local collection. The first faint beginnings of a career as a seaside resort were seen in the 1820s, when the lodging houses on Centre Cliff were built – but Southwold was always a quiet place, catering for persons of refinement with its numerous open 'greens', its small houses in flint and red brick, and its Georgian inns. Six 18-pounder cannons pointing out to sea from Gun Hill were put there in the 18th century, but have never been used. The fishing harbour is to the south, at the mouth of the River Blyth.

*The lighthouse rises among the houses on the cliff top*

### Battle in Sole Bay

In May 1672, during the wars against the Dutch, the allied English and French fleet put into Sole Bay, off Southwold, for fresh water. The commander-in-chief was the future James II, King Charles II's younger brother. In the night the Dutch navy appeared, under the great Admiral De Ruyter, and almost took the allies by surprise. Battle was joined by six o'clock in the morning, and the enemies pounded each other with terrible ferocity all day. James's flagship was so badly battered that he had to shift to another vessel, and in the evening was forced to move yet again. The *Royal James* was set alight by a fireship and blew up, and the English casualties were put at about 2500 men. Finally the Dutch withdrew, and both sides claimed the victory.

# INDEX